Front endpaper *Chinstrap penguins get their name from the distinctive black marking on the white feathers below their beaks.*

Opposite *Flamingoes live on the edge of the Rift Valley lakes in eastern Africa. The pink color comes from a microscopic organism which is part of the flamingo's diet.*

Overleaf *The edible frog is widespread throughout Europe, Asia and northern Africa.*

Contents page *Hippopotamuses are found in and around rivers in Africa. Their name means literally "river horse".*

Back endpaper *A cloud forest lit by the sun in Venezuela.*

WORLD OF NATURE

This book was devised and produced by
Multimedia Publications (UK) Ltd

Editor: Richard Rosenfeld
Assistant Editor: Sydney Francis
Production: Arnon Orbach
Design: Michael Hodson Designs
Maps: Janos Marffy
Picture research: Ethel Hurwicz and
          Moira Royce

First published in the United States of
America 1985 by

GALLERY BOOKS
An imprint of **W H SMITH PUBLISHERS INC.**,
112 Madison Avenue,
New York, NY 10016

ISBN 0-8317-3619-7

Reprinted 1988

Origination by The Clifton Studio Ltd, London
Printed in Italy by New Interlitho Spa

GALLERY BOOKS
An Imprint of W. H. Smith Publishers Inc.
112 Madison Avenue
New York City 10016

WORLD OF NATURE

ROBIN DUNBAR

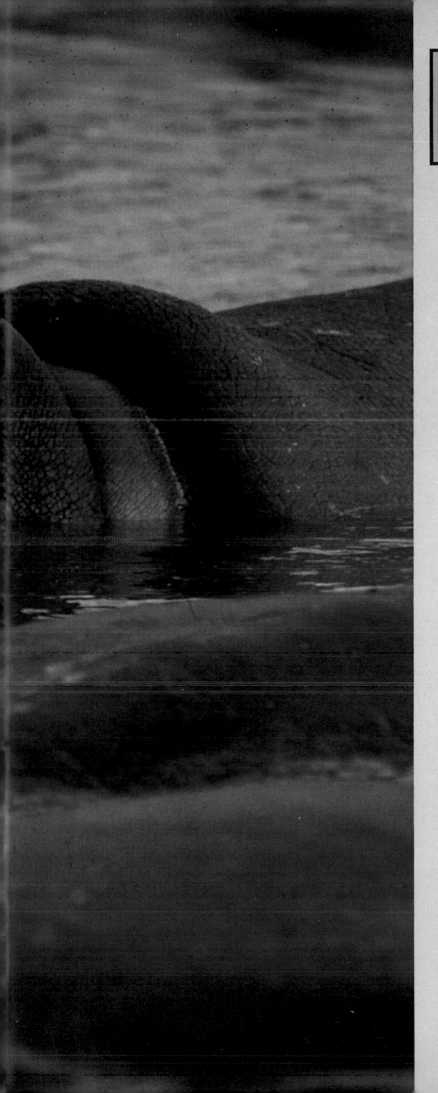

Contents

Africa

Two hundred million years ago Africa lay at the center of the world, the pivotal landmass in the ancient supercontinent of Pangaea. Gradually this great continent fractured and split apart, and the continents we know today slowly began to spread over the face of the planet. Though the movement was imperceptibly slow, the displacement of such massive blocks of the earth's crust inevitably created unbearable strains and tensions in the rocks, and these have left their mark on Africa ever since.

A huge scar runs down its eastern side, created by repeated cracking or "faulting" of the ancient rocks. Between the faults, giant blocks of the crust have dropped away to form the Great African Rift Valley. It runs for almost 2500 miles (4000 km) from Mozambique in the south to Ethiopia in the north, up the Red Sea (with straight, parallel sides created by Rift Valley faults) and on into Jordan.

Steam vents and volcanoes

The weakness in the earth's crust, caused by faulting, has resulted in extensive volcanic activity in and around the Rift Valley. Hot springs, steam vents and volcanoes litter its floor. Flows of jagged, solidified lava testify to the violence of their eruptions. Among the better known volcanic peaks are the giant snow-capped cones of Kilimanjaro – at 19 340 ft (5895 m) the continent's highest mountain – and Mt Kenya.

These mountain areas have luxurious forests of cedar and juniper on their lower slopes. Higher up, they give way to dense thickets of bamboo and then to forests of giant lichen-covered heather and St John's wort – small plants in Europe that here thrust their gnarled and twisting trunks more than 20 ft (6 m) into the air. On the highest reaches, just below the sterile snow-capped peaks, there are numerous moorlands dotted with giant lobelia and senecio.

A landscape of extremes

The Sahara is the largest desert in the world: its sheer size is difficult to comprehend. It occupies 3½ million square miles (9 million square km), an area roughly equivalent to that of the whole of Europe.

Within this vast region, the scenery ranges from the barren rocky plateaus of central Libya and the rugged mountains of the Tibesti and Hoggar ranges to the delicately shaded dunes of the great sand sea, blown into intricate patterns by the winds. The aridity is broken here and

The African elephant has an ingenious method of removing ticks. It squirts mud over itself and scrapes it off, with the parasites, when dry. Dust baths also help to keep numbers down.

there by the sudden lushness of scattered green oases.

With the exception of these mountains and oases, most of the Sahara remains uninhabited by man, but its apparent emptiness is deceptive. In the heat of the day, the desert is silent, but by night it rustles and hums with life. Insects and spiders scurry across the sand. Gerbils and jerboas, small kangaroo-like rodents, leap from one hole to another beneath scattered clumps of desert scrub. A sand viper buries itself in the sand so that only its eyes and snout show, patiently waiting for an unwary victim to pass within reach.

Survival
Life is a hard and dangerous business in these extreme conditions, where the lack of water is just one problem among many. Scimitar-horned oryx and fleet-footed gazelle have adapted to the desert so well that they manage without water altogether, extracting what little moisture they need from the sparse vegetation growing on rocky outcrops.

The hottest place on earth is the Danakil desert, which occupies the northern section of the Horn of Africa. The Dallol depression at its northern end traps the heat of the sun to generate an average year-round temperature of 94°F (34°C). Much of the Danakil lies below sea level, a furnace of unmitigated ferocity where incredibly beautiful crystalline salt deposits are created by evaporation from volcanic hot springs. Even larger rivers like the Awash lose themselves in the arid landscape, unable to find an exit into the nearby Red Sea.

Living fossil
At Africa's other extreme, on the southwest coast, lies a different kind of desert. This is the Namib, where the sea breezes bring in moist air to form a fog over the land, depositing a film of moisture on the arid soil. Plants that can absorb water directly from the air thrive here, including the "living fossil" *welwitschia*, a bizarre survivor from a distant era, whose relationship with other plants continues to puzzle botanists. Though it lives for up to 100 years, it produces just two leaves in its lifetime. These grow indefinitely, snaking and twisting their way over the shifting desert sands.

Africa is a land of superlatives, and the Nile is no exception. The longest river in the world, it covers a distance of 4000 miles (6500 km) from its source in Lake Victoria, through the eastern margins of the Sahara, to the Mediterranean Sea. Along its upper reaches in the Sudan, it waters grasslands that teem with wildlife. Here, antelope, buffalo, zebra and elephant graze in herds that far exceed those of the better known East African plains, where the animals are often outnumbered by tourists.

Savage predators
This is one of the last great wildlife sanctuaries in Africa where the great predators of the plains – lion and cheetah, hunting dog and hyena – still roam as freely as they did before the first European explorers arrived.

The Nile, in fact, is really two very different rivers – the Blue and White Niles – that meet in the middle of the Sudan to flow northwards through Egypt. The Blue Nile or Abbai ("father of waters") begins its life in Lake Tana, high up on the Ethiopian plateau. Swinging first south and then west in a great circular course, the river cuts down through the crumbling lavas of the plateau to emerge onto the Sudanese plain almost 5000 ft (1525 m) below. At its most impressive, it cuts a gorge more than 8 miles (13 km) wide and a mile deep.

Fossilized time
The precipitous streams that flow down into the Blue Nile from the Ethiopian plateau bring 70 per cent of the Nile's flood waters and many thousands of tons of rich volcanic topsoil, stripped from the gorge sides by these thundering torrents as they rip their way through fossilized time. They have created such deep and complex gorges in the plateau that, even today, much of it remains uncharted and inaccessible.

As it journeys towards the sea, the Nile deposits its load of fertile volcanic soil along its banks in lower Egypt, creating ideal conditions for agriculture. Each year when the Nile floods, the soil is replenished and revitalized. And so it has been for thousands of years, forming the basis of the ancient Egyptian civilization. The Nile has shaped history in a way that few other rivers have done.

Blocked channels
In contrast to the torrential Blue Nile, the middle reaches of the White Nile are a morass of swampy vegetation. In its meandering course across the southern Sudanese plains, the Nile creates the Sudd, an impenetrable papyrus reed swamp whose channels shift continually as the fast-growing clumps of water hyacinth choke first one and then another.

The White Nile loses nearly half the water brought from Uganda in these swamps through evaporation and seepage. It is such an unpredictable area that many who dared to enter it have failed to emerge at its further end. Even now, it remains an impassable barrier for river traffic, a waterlogged world with an exciting range of wildlife including Nile perch, crocodiles and beautiful water birds.

To the west of the Great Rift Valley and its flanking mountains lie the forests of the Congo basin and the equatorial belt. In the dense tracts of the Ituri and Congo forests live shy furtive creatures – delicate pygmy antelope, chameleons, brightly colored touracos that glide between the towering trees on stiff wings, the rare okapi discovered only as recently as 1900 and the endangered gorillas and smaller chimpanzees.

Forests and swamps
These often dark and impenetrable forests are drained by Africa's second longest river, the Congo, which flows westwards into the Atlantic. In some parts of its lower reaches, the river is 8 miles (13 km) wide.

Further to the south, beyond the intervening savanna grasslands, the Okavango swamp nestles into the northern edge of the Kalahari desert. It is fed by the Cubango river, draining southwards out of the Angolan hinterland. The swamps and the seasonally inundated mudflats provide an important refuge for wildlife in the arid Kalahari, a vast area of red sands and trackless thorn scrub. The Okavango is a region that is exceptionally rich in antelope and predators, as well as birds, crocodiles and hippo.

Lemur island
Madagascar was once part of the African mainland, but became separated from it about a hundred million years ago by the Mozambique Channel, a stretch of water 250 miles (400 km) wide. The island has remained a museum of living fossils that underwent their own idiosyncratic evolution at a time when momentous changes were taking place among the species on the mainland.

Much of the island's vegetation is unique, notably the weird cactus-like *diderea* forests of the south. Half of the island's 260 bird species occur nowhere else, while many of its fishes and reptiles, though essentially African in character, have evolved their own brilliant, and sometimes bizarre, appearances. Because the separation occurred before the great burgeoning of mammal species, there are few mammals on the island. Apart from its lemurs, Madagascar can claim only a handful of weasel-like civets, several dozen bats and a curious group of insect-eating tenrecs, none of whose 20-odd species are found anywhere else. But the island's real glory are its lemurs, a unique flourishing of the early primates that, on the mainland, gave rise to the monkeys and apes of today.

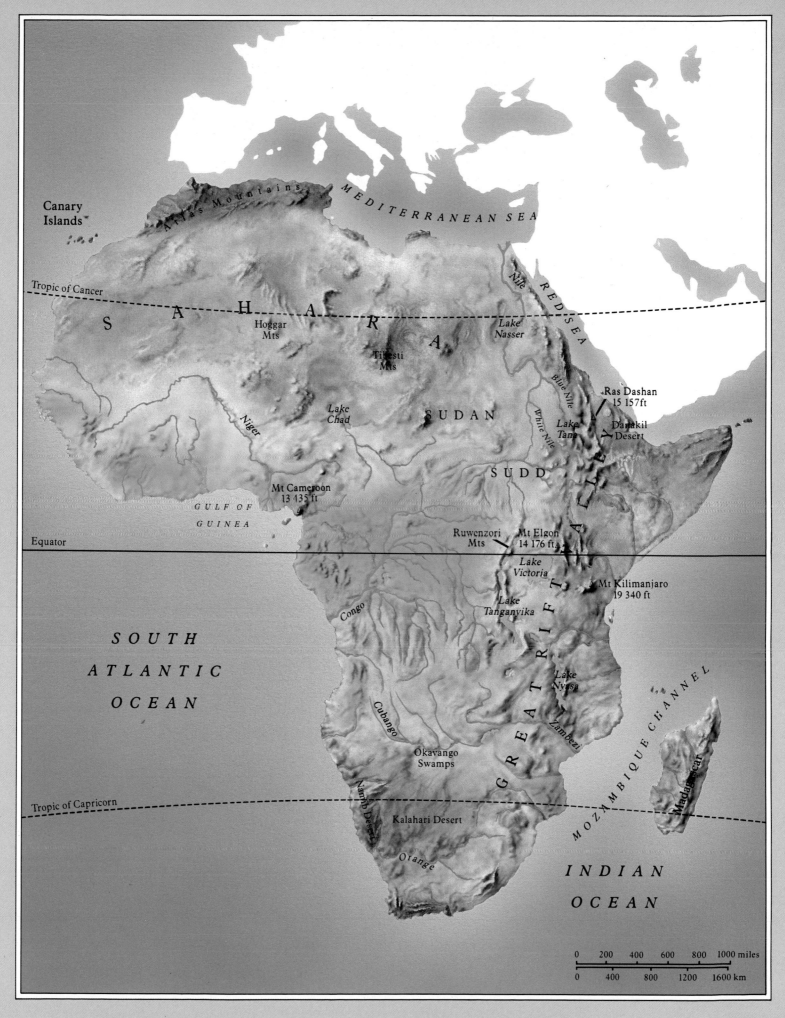

Canary
Islands

Atlas Mountains

MEDITERRANEAN SEA

Tropic of Cancer

S   A   H   A   R   A

Hoggar
Mts

Tibesti
Mts

Lake
Nasser

Nile

RED SEA

Blue Nile

Ras Dashan
15 157ft

White Nile

Lake
Tana

Danakil
Desert

Lake
Chad

SUDAN

Niger

SUDD

Mt Cameroon
13 435 ft

GULF OF
GUINEA

Ruwenzori
Mts

Mt Elgon
14 176 ft

Equator

Lake
Victoria

Mt Kilimanjaro
19 340 ft

Congo

Lake
Tanganyika

GREAT RIFT VALLEY

SOUTH

ATLANTIC

OCEAN

Lake
Nyasa

Cubango

Zambezi

MOZAMBIQUE CHANNEL

Okavango
Swamps

Madagascar

Namib Desert

Tropic of Capricorn

Kalahari Desert

Orange

INDIAN

OCEAN

| 0 | 200 | 400 | 600 | 800 | 1000 miles |

| 0 | 400 | 800 | 1200 | 1600 km |

The Savanna

Left *Hanging below its thundercloud, a rainstorm sweeps across the savanna grasslands. The rain can turn the parched plains green again almost overnight, bringing life back to the vegetation and stimulating dormant seeds to grow. Many herds of migratory antelope use the sight of a distant thunderstorm as a cue to head for fresh pastures, and will arrive in the wake of a storm to take advantage of the new grass.*

Below far left *Marabou storks cluster around an elephant in search of frogs and insects disturbed by the giant's feet.*
Marabous are among the commonest scavengers in Africa, stalking like undertakers in their tailcoats around carcasses.

Below center *The secretary bird is capable of moving with such lightning speed that it can out-maneuver, catch and eat even the deadliest snake. The bird owes its name to feathers which stick out like quill pens behind its "ears".*

Below *A carmine bee-eater hitches a ride on a kori bustard. As the bustard moves through the long grass on the open plains it sends insects flying from their hiding places which are promptly caught by the bee-eater.*

Left *Weighing in at only 10 lb (4.5 kg), the Kirk's dik-dik is one of the smallest antelopes in the world. They live in pairs occupying their own small territory and remain together for life. Always on the alert, dik-diks will flee rapidly and silently into the dense bush to escape their many predators.*

Right *Although many antelopes can survive without drinking for long periods, standing pools of water often attract them from far and wide. The antelopes look docile, but will fight over the last drops in the dry season. Here, a male kudu disturbs the smaller female impala.*

Below right *Zebra live in close-knit family units, each guarded by a stallion. Yet hooves can fly even among friends when the groups become too crowded. A zebra's stripes are unique to the individual, like giant "fingerprints", enabling each animal to be recognized by its pattern.*

Above *Once thought to live purely by scavenging from the kills of other predators, hyenas are in fact one of the most formidable hunters on the plains. Working together in packs, they can take on the largest species of animals with more success than even a pride of lions. Hunting expeditions begin with ritualized greeting and marking ceremonies that whip up excitement for the kill.*

However, even hyenas tend to be pestered by vultures. The birds' sharp eyes enable them to spot kills as they circle high is the sky. Here a frustrated hyena tries to drive off whitebacked vultures intent on gorging the remains of a zebra carcass.

Left *When a leopard makes a kill it drags the carcass to a suitable tree and hangs it there in a sort of "larder". Here it is safe from the attentions of marauding scavengers such as hyenas, and the leopard can return to a guaranteed supply of meat night after night.*

15

Elephants are the largest living land animals. They are among the most intelligent and sociable of all the species on earth, living in tightly knit groups that consist of closely related females and offspring. The mature males lead a more solitary life away from the female-dominated herds.

Elephants have just one enemy, man, who has decimated their numbers through his insatiable appetite for ivory.

Above *Three large females shelter a youngster against the raging torrent while crossing a dangerously swollen river.*

Right *The elephant's trunk is the most adaptable accessory in the animal world.*

Left *Cape buffalo are widely acknowledged as the most cunning and dangerous of all African animals, because their behavior is often completely unpredictable. Although the big mammals of the African plains no longer occur in the vast numbers they once did, buffalo still roam the savannas in massive herds many thousands strong.*

By the end of the dry season little remains to eat on the grasslands of the East African savannas, so the wildebeest set off on an annual migration. Gradually the small groups converge into large herds (top) in the search for fresh pastures.

As the wildebeest herds cross the plains, they sometimes find their way blocked by rivers.

When this happens they converge on traditional fording points (right).

The only way to cross a river flooded during the rainy season is by swimming. Here a young wildebeest leaps in while an adult looks on (above).

More wildebeest gather on the riverbank (overleaf), ready to plunge into the water, while vultures watch and wait hungrily.

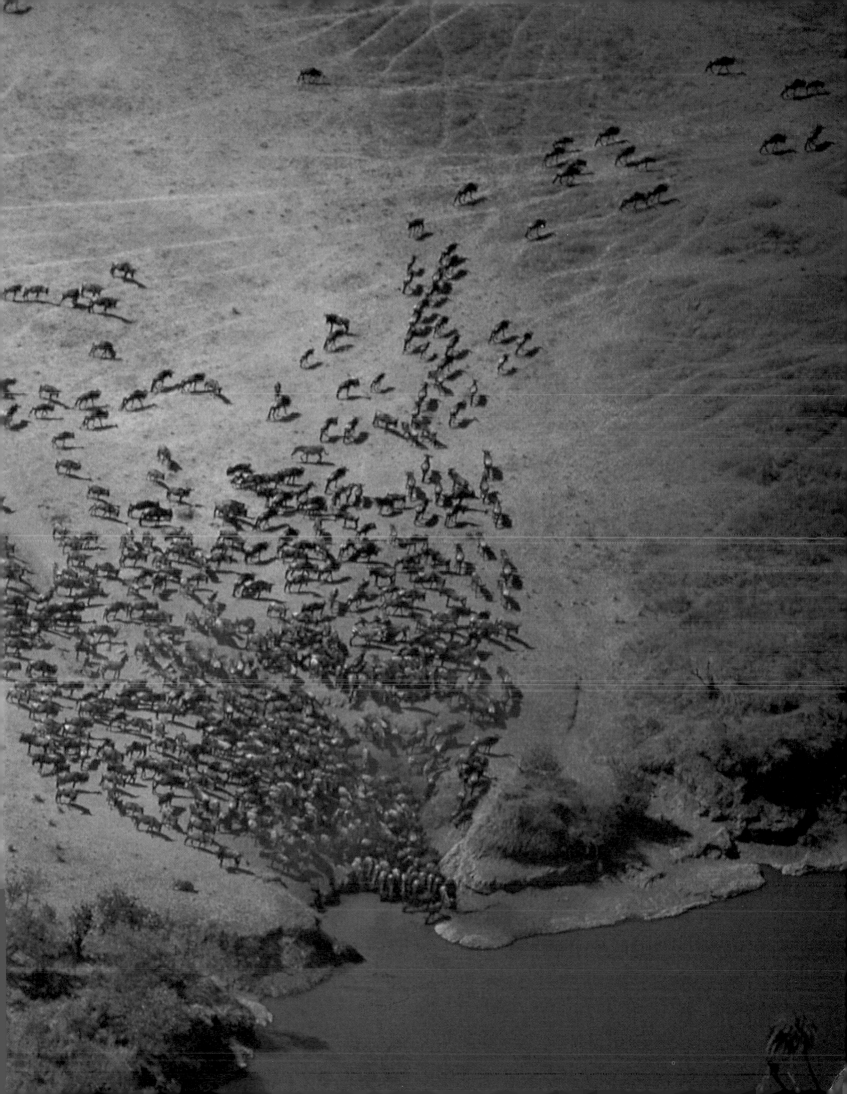

Right *Struggling up the steep bank on the far side, wildebeest fight their way to safety. Many are crushed and trampled to death during the desperate struggle.*

Below *Vultures and a marabou stork close in to gorge themselves.*

Far right *Other wildebeest, however, fail even to reach the far bank. They are washed down by flood water, their bloated bodies gathering in quiet backwaters.*

WEAVER BIRDS

Weaver birds are small grain-eating birds of the finch family. Their name derives from the way in which their nests are woven into intricate shapes. Weaver birds occur throughout Africa, as well as in Asia, and have occupied almost every habitat from rich rain forest to dry desert. Although species that live in forests are usually more solitary, those that live in open savanna habitats often form huge colonies; sometimes as many as one million birds may nest in a single tree.

Large colonies are of especial importance to weavers living in semi-desert areas where food is very patchily distributed, often at great distances from the colony. The colony acts as a center where birds can exchange information about food supplies. The birds forage outwards in different directions during the day. Those that found food on the previous day tend to leave the colony early in the morning and fly confidently off in the direction where they know they have found food, while the others that fared rather badly hang back to see where the successful birds go, and then follow.

Weaver birds build their nests in trees out of reach of predators. Some species hang the nest from the end of a fine branch, often over water, while others build them in thorn trees where vicious spines discourage animals from climbing up. The nests are woven mostly by the male from grass leaves and stalks, and in some species can be quite elaborate.

Right and inset above *Nests are usually hung from the branches of thorn trees in order to protect them from predators.*

Below *The Cape weaver bird which characteristically enters its nest upside down.*

Inset far right *A male weaver bird building his nest.*

Forests

Tropical forests are everywhere under threat. Each year, vast areas are cut down to satisfy an unending demand for timber, firewood and paper. Forest trees and plants have produced valuable products ranging from foods to medicines, and no one knows how many more such products still await discovery within the world's dwindling forests. But it is not only the trees that we lose when the forests go. Many rare species of animals live exclusively within their confines. Because they are often specialized forest-dwellers, many are unable to survive in the degraded open habitats that remain after the forests are cleared.

Right *Confined to the forest remnants of Africa's equatorial west coast, the mandrill is the rarest of all the large African monkeys. It lives in small bands that wander widely through the forest in search of fruits. Although the male's gaudy face is quite unique among the mammals, the reason for its being so colorful has not yet been determined.*

Far right *One of the most widespread of all the primates, baboons occur in all habitats from rainforest through to arid thornscrub. Baboons are among the most social of all the monkeys and apes, living in troops of up to 100 individuals.*

Below *The inquisitive and highly sociable chimpanzee lives in loosely organized communities in which personal friendships play an important part. But its survival hinges on the continued existence of the dwindling forests of central and western Africa.*

Above *Chameleons are famous for their ability to change color to suit the background. With eyes that can swivel independently forwards and backwards, a chameleon creeps up on unsuspecting prey with slow, deliberate movements. Once within range, its telescopic tongue darts out to snare the prey on its sticky tip. Chameleons usually feed on small insects like flies, but can take on ones as large as this locust.*

Far left *The praying mantis is the most patient of the insect hunters and waits, completely still, for an unwary insect to stray too close. Then it strikes like lightning with its forelegs to capture its prey. This one has caught a cricket.*

Left *A crab spider sets about eating a moth. Such a large prey will last for some time.*

Deserts

Above *When enough rain falls, grass springs up as though from nowhere, attracting locusts that swarm across the landscape devouring all vegetation in their path.*

Above left *Deserts occur wherever the rainfall is too meager to allow plant life to flourish on a permanent basis. Desert landscapes can vary from sand dunes to rocky outcrops and barren mountain ranges. Yet water plays an important part in desert life. In the Sahara wadis are the dried up beds of seasonal rivers that have cut into the sand.*

Left *The presence of permanent waterholes where underground springs emerge can result in deserts unexpectedly rich in wildlife. Here a herd of zebra visits a desert waterhole in Namibia. The landscape is powdered white by encrusted salts formed as the water evaporates during the long dry season.*

Above *The egg-eating snake lives mainly on birds' eggs. By gradually working its mouth and body around the egg, the snake forces the egg into its stomach where the shell is broken by the contraction of powerful muscles. Since snakes can unhinge their lower jaws to enlarge their gape, even the largest eggs pose few problems.*

Left *Against the red sands of the Namib desert, a chameleon catches a harvester termite on its sticky telescopic tongue and flicks it back into its mouth.*

Above left *Scorpions mainly feed on other insects which they catch with their formidable claws before stinging them to death. Prior to an attack the scorpion arches its tail over its head ready to deliver a paralyzing sting. Here a tiny drop of venom, sqeezed out from poison glands, glistens ominously on the needle-sharp tip. The scorpion will then inject a powerful digestive enzyme into the insect, turning its internal tissues into liquid. Finally, the scorpion sucks it dry, leaving only the empty exoskeleton.*

Above *In deserts, where prey animals may be few and far between, a snake must use all its cunning if it is to eat. In the stony floor of a dried-up gully, a Peringuey's viper lies concealed. Its tail lures birds and small mammals within easy reach of the venomous fangs.*

Left *This horned adder is also known as a sidewinder because of its extraordinary way of moving up the slippery slopes of sand dunes.*

Right *One of the deadliest snakes in Africa is the puff adder, which feeds mostly on small rodents. But its reluctance to move out of the way when approached results in its delivering a formidable and frequently fatal bite to anyone luckless enough to step on it*

Rivers, Lakes and Swamps

Left *In the highlands of Ethiopia, the Blue Nile emerges from its source in Lake Tana at an altitude of 7000 ft (2134 m). It flows over a series of falls to gouge out a canyon, in some places nearly a mile deep, before it joins the White Nile in the Sudan. During the rainy season the Blue Nile's coffee-colored water contains rich volcanic soils washed down from the Ethiopian hills to be deposited on the Nile delta in Egypt.*

Below and bottom *The Nile's most famous inhabitants, its crocodiles, are among the largest reptiles in the world. They prey on the giant perch and catfish that abound in the river, as well as on any antelope or other animal that ventures too far in when drinking from its banks.*

Like all reptiles, crocodiles hatch from eggs as fully formed miniature adults. They still need their parents' protection, however, and an adult crocodile will carry its babies in its mouth from one spot to another.

37

Above *The graceful crowned crane is more often found on the marshes and lakeside grasslands, where it feeds on all kinds of small animals from frogs to rodents.*

Left *The lakes that litter the floor of the Great Rift Valley provide some of the most spectacular bird-watching in the world. Flamingoes occur in such numbers that they often create pink "rings" around the edges of the lakes.*
  The flamingo is a filter feeder: it uses its powerful tongue muscles to force 30 gallons (135 l) of water a day through a series of fine filters in its tubular beak. These trap vast numbers of tiny shrimps and algae that live in the alkaline lake water. The pink color of the flamingo's feathers is caused by one of the microscopic organisms that it eats.

Top left *Pelicans fish in flocks that drive fish schools ahead of them. They use their leathery beak pouches to scoop up great mouthfuls of fish.*

Above *The Cape pangolin is one of four species of scaly anteater found in Africa. These curious reptile-like mammals are toothless and use their long sticky tongues to scoop ants and termites into their mouths.*

Right *The renowned Okavango swamps of Botswana provide a haven for wildlife on the northern edge of the sun-baked Kalahari desert.*

Below right *The boomslang is one of the deadliest snakes in Africa, spending most of its time in trees and bushes through which it can move with a speed and grace matched by few other snakes. It feeds mainly on birds, reptiles (like this chameleon) and the small mammals that live in trees.*

Mountains

Above *Ethiopia's Simen Mountains were formed by an outpouring of lava from a massive volcanic center that never actually erupted. Later upheavals in the Earth's crust resulted in one section being raised up to form the mile-high escarpment face of the mountain chain. Below the main escarpment the soils have been eroded away to reveal the hard plugs of the old volcanic blow-holes, now clearly visible in the middle distance as steep-sided flat-topped mountains.*

Opposite *The twin-peaked Kilimanjaro, at 19 340 ft (5895 m) Africa's highest mountain, is permanently snow-capped, but the crater on its large peak clearly reveals its volcanic origins. The high mountains of Africa generally are volcanic in origin.*

Right *Plants often grow to giant size at high altitudes. In the mist-shrouded Ruwenzori Mountains, these lobelia have grown huge seed spikes to a height of 10 ft (3m) or more. The densely packed leaves at the base provide a warm microcosm for a whole world of insects that would otherwise be unable to survive the cold nights at such high altitudes.*

MADAGASCAR

A remarkable flowering of primitive primate species occurred on the island of Madagascar after it had separated from the African mainland some 60 million years ago. Nobody knows for sure how representatives of the primitive primates, widespread throughout the continent, came to be on the island, but one theory put forward is that they drifted across the channel of water on floating vegetation.

Once on the island, however, the lemurs found an almost deserted paradise. The result was a dramatic increase in numbers and the colonizers soon began to evolve and diversify into new species. As recently as 2000 years ago there were some 33 living varieties of lemur. Fossil evidence suggests that in prehistoric times there were many other species, including the giant hadrolemur.

After the arrival of man on the island, many species died out. Now only 19 remain, and many of these are threatened with imminent extinction. Those that survived are mostly tree-dwelling species that live in the more remote forests.

The living species are typified by the true lemurs, which include species such as the ringtailed lemur, the gentle lemur and the sportive lemur that live in groups of 10-20 animals. The lemur family also includes a number of solitary nocturnal species like the dwarf lemur, the mouse lemur and the diminutive aye-aye, most of which keep their young in nests in hollow trees. Another group of lemurs includes the sifaka, the largest of the living lemurs, and the indri, whose eerie wails terrified the early human settlers on the island.

Main picture *The huge forests on the northern coast have been almost completely destroyed by man.*

Top left *The tiny mouse lemur is only active at night.*

Below left *The sifaka is the largest living lemur.*

Above *Ringtailed lemurs use their long tails to waft scent at their enemies to drive them away.*

Europe

Europe is the second smallest of the continents, and consists essentially of two large peninsulas jutting out from the great Russian plain, one being Scandinavia and the other the main west European block. In reality, these two peninsulas are the visible remnants of a drowned continent that once extended into the North Sea as far as Iceland. The English Channel is no more than a submerged river valley between the higher ground of the English and French hills.

Across the north of Europe lie ancient granite mountains, running through Ireland and Scotland and on to Scandinavia. The inundated mountains on the coastline form the deep sheer-sided fjords of Scandinavia and a chain of craggy islands off the coast. These islands stretch from Spitsbergen in the north, down through the Lofoten islands and the Shetlands and Orkneys to the Hebrides off the west coast of Scotland.

Great mountain ranges

Further south, the more recent fold mountains of the Alps system extend magnificently across the continent. These include the Pyrenees and Sierra Nevada mountains of Spain in the west, and the Carpathians and Balkan mountains in the east. Sandwiched between the two great blocks of mountains lies the vast European plain that spreads eastwards as far as the Ural Mountains in central Russia. Finally, at the southern limits of Europe, are the drier hilly lands bordering the Mediterranean Sea, where a different kind of vegetation takes over, and the influence of the nearby African continent can be seen in the indigenous wildlife.

Influence of Ice Age

To the southeast the jagged northern highlands give way to the great north European plain than runs from the East Anglian coast of Britain, through Holland and Denmark, across the northern parts of Germany and Poland, and into Finland and Russia. In Scandinavia and northern Russia there are numerous lakes dotting the landscape, some of considerable size. Most of these owe their origins to the glacial moraines – accumulations of rock debris left behind by the glaciers as they began to retreat towards the end of the last Ice Age. These moraines blocked natural drainage lines to create lakes, often of spectacular beauty.

Bordering many of the lakes are extensive pine forests, and these are one of the last refuges of the wolverine. The largest member of the weasel family, the wolver-

Gannets are found on islands in the North Atlantic, where they breed in rookeries on sheer sea cliffs. They fly out from these roosts over the gray waves in search of fish.

ine is more often heard than seen, as its piercing scream echoes among the trees. It feeds on rodents, birds and invertebrates in summer but has also been known to kill reindeer. In winter, carrion forms a large part of its diet and it travels great distances in search of carcasses.

North Sea mudflats
On the coasts of the North Sea, the flatness of the land results in low-lying mudflats that extend along the coasts of Holland and eastern England, often creating salt-marsh habitats on sheltered tidal estuaries. These lonely, windswept areas are vitally important feeding grounds for huge flocks of shorebirds. Dunlin, stilts, redshank, oystercatchers, stints, sanderling, curlew and ruff are among the many species that probe the mudflats for worms and shellfish, while terns and gulls wheel overhead.

From October to March their numbers swell with the arrival of impressive flocks of large herbivorous birds, such as brent goose and Bewick's swan, escaping the Arctic winter to graze on the salt-marsh plants of the estuaries.

Wolves and lynx
In the far north of Scandinavia and Russia, beyond the Arctic Circle, the winter temperatures are too low to permit anything except tundra vegetation to grow. Native animals include reindeer and lemmings, while moose and lynx frequent the forests that border the tundra zone. Stalking through the trees alone at night, the lynx moves on thickly furred, outsize paws that act like snowshoes to prevent it from sinking into the drifts. This is also the last habitat in Western Europe of wild wolves.

South of the coniferous forest belt, in the warmer climate of the European plain, a parallel strip of deciduous forest extends across the continent. Typically made up of beech and oak, it includes a number of other species such as ash, lime, birch and elm. These forests often have dense undergrowth that attracts an abundant bird life and a variety of mammals, including species like red squirrels, roe and fallow deer, foxes and badgers. Wild boar and wolf were once common too, but these are now practically extinct.

The forgotten sea
South of the forest belt, Russia suffers from the extremes of climate that often afflict the centers of large landmasses – cold winters and hot summers, combined with low rainfall. These extremes of temperature support straggling woodland or grassland vegetation, depending on the rainfall. In southern Russia this climate has produced steppe grassland, now the expansive agricultural heartland of the Ukraine bordering the Black Sea. Further to the east, where the annual rainfall is less than 10 in (25 cm), semi-desert spreads down into the great basin of the Caspian Sea.

The Caspian is the largest of all the lakes in the world by a very considerable margin: it is 5½ times the size of Lake Superior, its nearest rival. Once the eastern arm of the Mediterranean Sea, it lies in a relatively flat-bottomed depression, its surface some 85 ft (26 m) below sea level and threatening to fall still lower because of climatic change and lack of rainfall to replace the constant depletion of its waters by irrigation programs.

The lake is well stocked with fish, lobsters and sponges, many of which occur nowhere else. The water, however, is brackish, and many species, like the local herring, have distinct marine affinities. The Caspian Sea also has its own species of seal which, like the seals of Lake Baykal far to the east, exhibit similarities to the seals of the Arctic Ocean.

Islands in the sky
The Alps are the high point of Europe, with many peaks lying above 12 000 ft (3660 m). At such altitudes, the peaks are inevitably snow-bound throughout the year. It has been estimated that the Alps contain over 1200 glaciers and ice fields.

The Alps form a natural barrier between the Baltic and the Mediterranean parts of Europe, and plants from each of these areas are found alongside the characteristic alpine vegetation. Above the tree line, the mountain passes and valleys are carpeted in a profusion of flowers during the spring, including saxifrages, azaleas, dwarf willows, primulas, gentians and, of course, the edelweiss.

Curiously, the edelweiss is not really an alpine plant at all, though it is undoubtedly the one plant most closely identified with the mountains. In fact, it is really a plant of the Siberian steppe, far to the east. Its presence in the Alps is probably due to the steppe-like conditions that prevailed throughout Europe during the warmer, drier periods between successive Ice Ages; subsequently, as the forests began to grow on the lower slopes of the mountains once more, the edelweiss was pushed further and further towards the summits, where it now lives.

Alpine refuge
Although there are relatively few species of animals that are peculiar to the Alps, a great many varieties that were once widespread throughout surrounding lower lands have found a haven there in the face of man's encroachment on their habitats. Among these are such species as the lynx, brown bear, stonemarten, stoat (or ermine) and Alpine marmot.

Other species, like the graceful ibex and the chamois (a goat-antelope), are outposts of groups that are widely represented throughout the mountains and deserts of the Middle East and the Himalayan region. In the cold of winter the chamois move down from the peaks to coniferous forest while the marmot hibernates in a communal burrow for six to eight months.

Ecological islands
From an ecological point of view, high mountains often act like oceanic islands. Species that reach them during periods when climatic or other conditions permit large-scale movements soon find themselves trapped there when conditions change again. Unable to tolerate the conditions then existing in the intervening areas, they are cut off from their ancestral stock, and may begin to evolve into new species.

A particularly clear instance of this is provided by the numerous butterfly species that inhabit the Alps, only one third of which are found in the surrounding lowlands. Butterflies are also favored by the comparative dearth of other insects competing for the same food sources.

The Mediterranean
South of the great southern European mountain chains lies the hot and relatively dry coastal zone of the Mediterranean basin. To the ancient civilizations of Europe, this sea stood at the center of the world, a belief still reflected in its name, meaning literally "middle of the earth".

The rugged, broken landscape that surrounds the Mediterranean owes much of its characteristic form to its position as a buffer zone between the African and European continents. At the eastern end, in particular, the mountains come right down to the sea, forming steep cliffs that plunge straight into the Mediterranean's blue waters. The Balkan coastline along the Adriatic and Aegean Seas is extensively broken up, with a great many rocky islands lying offshore.

Of all the European landscapes it is, perhaps, hardest of all to envisage that of the Mediterranean as once being covered by trees; but long ago it was thickly forested. Only a few isolated groves of holm oak, cork oak, and the aleppo pine have escaped clearance, but these still harbor a rich wildlife. Cicadas, whose shrill call is so evocative of the region, feed on the trees' sap, and on the woodland floor the wild boar, ancestor of the domestic pig, uses its long snout to dig for roots and tubers.

NORTH
POLE

ARCTIC OCEAN

Arctic Circle

Spitsbergen
Islands

Lofoten
Islands

Iceland

NORWEGIAN
SEA

NORTH

ATLANTIC

OCEAN

Faroe
Islands

Shetland
Islands

Hebrides

Orkney
Islands

NORTH

SEA

BALTIC SEA

Lake
Peipus

URAL MOUNTAINS

Ural

ENGLISH CHANNEL

Seine

Rhein

Elbe

Oder

Dnepr

Volga

Loire

BAY OF
BISCAY

Rhône

A L P S

Po

Carpathian Mountains

CASPIAN SEA

Pyrenees

Danube

BLACK SEA

Caucasus Mountains

Tagus

Mont Blanc
15 771 ft

ADRIATIC SEA

BALKAN PENINSULA

Guadalquivir

Balearic
Islands

Sardinia

AEGEAN
SEA

Sicily

Crete

Cyprus

M E D I T E R R A N E A N   S E A

0	200	400 miles

0	400	800 km

ATLANTIC ISLAND ROOKERIES

The remote islands scattered along the north-west coast of Europe have become havens for seabirds, many of whom find safety for their eggs and young chicks on the steep sea cliffs of islands like the St Kilda group and the solitary pinnacle of Rockall far out in the Atlantic to the west of Scotland. With no land predators to disturb their breeding colonies and few humans on these remote islands, the birds often breed in very large numbers. The sea cliffs, some of which rise more than 1000 ft (300 m) vertically out of very rough seas, are a major breeding ground for fulmars, razorbills and kittiwakes who nest on narrow ledges, while puffins and shearwaters burrow into the turf above. Gannets return to their colonies on these islands each year to roost on the cliffs. The open oceans supply all their food: the exploding plume of foam as a gannet plunges headfirst into the waves from a 100 ft (30 m) vertical power dive is one of the most spectacular sights on the European coast. Gray and common seals haul out of the water to bask in the sunshine on the rocky foreshore, calling to one another with their hauntingly plaintive cries. They gather in their hundreds on suitable beaches to form noisy breeding colonies in which the males fight out their territorial claims in bloody contests.

Above *A gannet guards its fluffy chick on its nest.*

Right *Puffins dig burrows in which to nest.*

Opposite *The kittiwake chooses perilous sites for its nest.*

Inset *A shag prepares to defend its chick against an intruder.*

The Coastline

Main picture *The Giant's Causeway, off the coast of Northern Ireland, is one of the most curious natural features in the British Isles. It forms a promontory 300 ft (90 m) long made up of a large number of six-sided columns of hard basalt rock, some rising to heights of 20 ft (6 m).*

Bottom left *The turnstone breeds around the Baltic and winters on the coasts of southern Europe and the British Isles. The bird gets its name from the way it turns stones over with its beak in order to search for sand-hoppers and other insects hiding beneath.*

Above *During storms the powerful Atlantic waves roll in to smash against the rugged headlands of Europe's western coast. Bays and hidden caves of spectacular beauty are formed through the gradual erosion of the rock.*

Mountains

Right *The chamois, a goat-antelope distantly related to the North American Rocky Mountain goat, has been forced to ever higher altitudes by human encroachment, and now ekes out a precarious existence along the snow line in the Alps.*

Below *The magnificent Aiguille d'Argentiere, a 12 795 ft (3900 m) peak in the French Alps.*

Far right *This spectacular view of the Matterhorn, which rises to a height of 14 678 ft (4500 m), illustrates why it is one of the most difficult Alpine mountains to climb.*

Main picture *In the western Pyrenees the Vignemale glacier winds its way down between the saw-toothed peaks, the surface strippled by the wind. Lying to the west of the Alps, the Pyrenees mark the borderland between France and Spain. Although not physically connected to them, the Pyrenees were formed at the same time as the Alps, and by the same subterranean movements.*

Inset left *High up on a mountain crag a pair of griffon vultures keep watch over the surrounding countryside for signs of carrion. These massive birds are usually found cruising effortlessly on outspread wings above the valleys.*

Inset right *A male ibex using its horn to scratch itself. Now more common in the Alps than the Pyrenees, these wild relatives of the goat have fine sets of majestic horns. The marked ridges ensure that, during a fierce butting fight, these extremely dangerous weapons "lock" against an opponent's, instead of glancing off and damaging the adversary's skull. These contests usually take place in the breeding season.*

Above *Where rivers pass through areas of soft limestone they often carve out underground channels, and may not re-emerge for many miles. In Spain's Ordessa National Park this river has gouged a deep channel and appears to flow from the very rockface itself.*

Left *The Dolomites make up the eastern arm of the Alps. Formed from a particularly hard type of rock, they are renowned for their rugged angular peaks. The fortress-like rocks shown here are known as "Tre Cime". The massive scale of their size is indicated by the hut at their foot.*

BIRD MIGRATION

Many species of European birds migrate southwards to over-winter along the Mediterranean or further south still in Africa, thereby avoiding the rigors of the northern winter. Great flocks of cranes, storks, geese, swallows, starlings, wheatears and a host of other species can be seen winging their way southwards in the autumn and northwards again in the spring. Most of the birds are channeled down through three routes across the Mediterranean: over Spain and the Italian peninsula or through the Balkans *(see map opposite)* to avoid having to cross wide stretches of open sea. The red arrowheads indicate the winter habitats of many of the migratory species, while the blue tails show their summer ranges.

Below *The Arctic tern often spends the summers in the Arctic and the winters in the Antarctic, whereas the nightingale* (inset below) *spends its summers in Europe and its winters in northern Africa.*

Far right *Greylag geese overwinter on the Spanish peninsula and,* **right,** *knots (members of the Sanderling family) spend the winter along the coasts of Britain and southern Europe.*

Woods and Moors

Above *Now mainly confined to the pine forests of the far north, the European lynx was once an important predator throughout the continent. The lynx's large thickly furred paws are ideal for moving across the deep snow drifts of the northern winter in the hunt for prey.*

Right *With a rime of hoar-frost accentuating its winter starkness, an English oak wood harbors a wealth of birds and mammals.*

Far right *Owls patrol the woods at night, searching with blazing eyes for prey. The radiating feathers round the owl's face act rather like a dish reflector, enabling the predator to detect even the slightest sound of creatures scurrying through the undergrowth.*

Main picture *The beechwoods
that extend right across the center
of Europe from the British Isles
into Russia are among the most
productive forests in the world.
The fruit, known as beechmast,
occurs in vast quantities providing
a rich source of food for millions
of seed-eating birds like titmice
and nuthatches. Many large
mammals like deer and wild boar
also feast on the fallen fruit. Even
humans have been known to eat
it during times of famine.*

Far left *A pair of beautiful
nymphalid butterflies mate
on the tip of a flower.*

Above *The Large Blue butterfly is
unique in that its larva has a
symbiotic relationship with
Myrmica ants.
 During the first three stages of
its life, the larva behaves like a
typical caterpillar and feeds on
plants, mainly wild thyme. When
it enters the last stage, however,
the larva suddenly stops eating
and begins to wander. At the same
time, a gland on its abdomen
begins to secrete a honey-like
liquid that attracts the ants which
drink the "honey".
 The larva allows an ant to
carry it off to its nest. There,
in exchange for shelter, the
caterpillar continues to provide its
hosts with "honey", but eats the
tiny ant larvae while doing so.
Since the caterpillar even pupates
in the ants' nest the butterfly has
to crawl out through the narrow
tunnels of the nest to reach the
open air and freedom.*

Above *During mating, the male red damselfly uses special pincers on the tip of his abdomen to grip the female by the back of the neck, thereby helping her to reach up to collect sperm from a receptacle on his thorax.*

Right *The male midwife toad carries spawn in strings wrapped around his back legs until the tadpoles are ready to hatch.*

Far right *The dragonfly's delicate transparent wings hardly seem to justify its reputation as one of the strongest fliers among the insects. It is a fearsome hunter and catches smaller insects in mid-air.*

Life hangs by a delicate thread for small mammals and birds, particularly during the winter. At this time of year, those creatures that neither migrate nor hibernate provide the main food source for larger predators, and few survive to the spring.

Above *The harvest mouse's nest is suspended from a bunch of corn stalks to keep it hidden. But there is little the mice can do to protect their young once the nest has been found by an alert weasel.*

Right *The red fox is the only large predator that is still common in Europe. In recent years it has even begun to live in the suburbs of large cities.*

Far right *The wild cat may have been the ancestor of the modern domestic cat. Now, however, it barely survives on the edge of civilization.*

With its shrill cry and striking livery of orange, blue and black, the kingfisher is unmistakable as it hovers over rivers or perches on an overhanging branch, watching the running water below for the tell-tale signs of movement made by the small fish and crustaceans on which it feeds.

A sudden dive launches it into the water in pursuit of its prey and once back on its perch it tosses the fish into the air to catch and swallow it in one deft movement. If the fish is too large to swallow in one piece, the bird will take it over to a rock and pound it into more manageable proportions.

The kingfisher builds its nest out of regurgitated fish bones at the end of a deep burrow tunneled into the river bank. Here, the female lays her translucent eggs in batches of up to six.

Above *Known as the "Monarch of the Glen", the red deer is Scotland's most common large mammal.*
This male is making it quite clear that this is his territory. Males assess each other's fighting prowess by roaring at each other: only if the males match each other's roaring abilities will they resort to fighting with their antlers.

Main picture *Under somber granite hills Scotland's ancient moorlands lie in their winter colors of yellow and brown. In spring they are bright with royal purple when the ling and heather burst into flower.*

Far left *A female crab spider rests on the purple flowers of a cross-leaved heath plant.*

THE CAMARGUE

The River Rhône flows out into the Mediterranean on the south coast of France and forms an extensive delta covering an area of some 200 square miles (520 sq km). Known as the Camargue, this vast expanse of shallow lagoons and reed-covered swamps provides an important haven for wildlife in a continent increasingly devoid of wilderness areas.

Another large area of swamp occurs on the southwest coast of Spain. Here, the delta of the Guadalquivir River opens out into the Atlantic Ocean on the Cote de Doñana, creating a 600 square mile (1600 sq km) area of swampland known as Las Marismas. Now a National Park, it is one of the last great wildernesses in Europe.

These desolate areas are the refuges for sizeable populations of Europe's dwindling wild mammals. The Camargue is famous for its wild white horses and black bulls, while the Guadalquivir delta has substantial populations of fallow deer, wild boar, badgers, mongoose and Spanish lynx.

But the real glory of these wetlands is their bird life. Such vast areas of water inevitably attract thousands of water birds. The huge spreading crown on the centuries-old cork trees of the Doñana are used as nest sites by spoonbills, hundreds of which crowd onto the branches once the chicks have hatched out.

The richness of the shallow reedbeds and lagoons attract a host of wading birds. In the Marismas, the rare purple heron waits patiently in the shallows for fish to swim within reach of its spear-like bill. The Camargue is particularly famous for its pink-tinged flamingos, of which it has the largest breeding colony in Europe. Little egrets, terns, plovers and curlews stalk across the sand dunes and the mudflats, while the secretive purple gallinule can only be located by its trumpet-like call.

Millions of ducks and geese winter in these areas while on migration from their northern breeding grounds. No less than 80 per cent of all the European greylag geese are said to winter on the Cote de Doñana. Many of the species that winter further to the south in Africa stop off in the swamps of the Marismas to restore their fat reserves for the long migration ahead.

The southern European wetlands are under permanent threat from development as the increasing demands of industrial societies encroach on their edges. The continued survival of these fragile habitats will ultimately depend on our ability to prevent pollution destroying their value as wildlife refuges.

Main picture *The tidal reed-swamps of the Camargue are a corner of Europe still untouched by modern civilization.*

Spoonbills (top), *herons* (center) *and wild horses* (below) *are among the many species for which the area is famous.*

North America

North America is dominated by two imposing chains of mountains running down the east and west sides of the continent. The eastern mountains, the Appalachian chain and the Allegheny Mountains, are the older. Smaller than the sawtooth giants of the Rocky Mountains to the west, they are the heavily eroded stumps of an old mountain system that was later lifted up and deformed by powerful geological forces at work beneath the surface. With altitudes that rarely exceed 6000 ft (1830 m), their vegetation is generally temperate in character. Deciduous forests and woodlands of birches, poplars, willows and oaks grace their slopes, and are renowned for the richness of their autumn colors.

The west coast mountains are of rather different origin. They are the product of relatively recent upheavals of the land that resulted from a dramatic collision between the continent's west coast and the submerged floor of the Pacific Ocean. As the American continental plate reared up over the Pacific Ocean floor, its edges crumpled to produce the great ranges of the Rocky Mountain chain that stretch from Alaska south to Mexico.

Rocky Mountain grizzlies
The highest part is the Alaskan Range where Mt McKinley reaches a height of 20 320 ft (6194 m) above sea level. Its glistening glaciers and cascades provide a dramatic backdrop to the stark Alaskan scenery. Throughout their range, the lower slopes of the Rockies support dense forests of pine and fir. Deer and grizzly bear range through the forests, while Rocky Mountain goats and bighorn sheep graze the open grasslands above the tree line.

Between the eastern and western mountain chains lie the Great Plains, an area of monotonously flat land 1500 miles (2415 km) wide that runs down from northernmost Canada right through into the central United States. Vast herds of bison and deer once roamed these plains in their great annual migrations. Although the bison are all but extinct, there are still significant numbers of caribou and moose amid the crystalline lakes of the far north of Canada.

Caribou migration
From here, the Barren Ground caribou embark on an annual migration that takes them 500 miles (800 km) southwards to escape the rigors of the polar winter. Each year, they have followed the same tracks through the dense coniferous

The Alaskan brown bear has become skilled at catching salmon as they swim up-river to spawn.

forests so that the rock has been worn away to depths of 2 ft (60 cm) or more.

Three major river systems begin on the Great Plains: the Mackenzie flows north to empty into the Arctic above Alaska, the St Lawrence drains eastwards from the Great Lakes to the north Atlantic, and the Mississippi runs southwards into the Gulf of Mexico. All three owe their present size to the effects of the Ice Age when glaciers rolled down from the Arctic, blocking rivers and diverting them from their ancient outlets to the sea so that they were forced to become tributaries of the major river systems.

Lakeside wildlife
The ice sheets were also responsible for many of the lakes – some of them covering huge areas – that are so characteristic of the Mackenzie and St Lawrence river basins. Immense flocks of wildfowl descend onto these lakes to feed and roost at the end of their long spring migrations.

Towards the northeast, the land gives way to a seascape of scattered islands of all shapes and sizes. These are the tips of ancient mountain peaks, all that remains of the continent's eastern end after the land surface had been tipped downwards into the sea to form a vast continental shelf. Known as the Grand Banks, it stretches out into the Atlantic for 500 miles (800 km) with depths no greater than 600 ft (183 m).

Fishing grounds
The shallowness of that submerged corner of the continent is responsible for the excellent fishing grounds that lie off the Newfoundland and New England coasts. Humpback whales return each summer to these waters to gorge themselves on the shoals of tiny creatures that come inshore to spawn.

Beyond the Arctic Circle lie the icebound islands of the Canadian Arctic archipelago, while to their east Greenland stands on an extension of the North American continental shelf.

This huge island is permanently icebound, with 85 per cent of its land surface covered by an ice sheet which is estimated to be some 6000 ft (1830 m) thick in the center of the island. Only a narrow coastal strip becomes free from ice during the summer months, though even then the climate is so cool and unpredictable that few species can survive.

Erik the Red
The island owes its implausible name to Erik the Red, a Viking adventurer who discovered it towards the end of the tenth century. Endeavoring to attract other settlers, he deliberately chose a name that painted an unrealistically cheerful picture of its environment.

Yet Greenland is not without its native fauna and flora. There are some 390 species of plants, about 50 of which were probably introduced from Europe by the Vikings during their occupation of the island between the eleventh and the fourteenth centuries.

Many of the Arctic mammals from mainland North America live here, including musk ox, lemmings, caribou, wolf and polar bears, while the walrus, several whales, and at least six species of seals are found offshore.

This is also an important area for birds: the northeast coast is a major breeding ground for barnacle and pinkfoot geese from Europe, and there are some 60 species of birds, half of which are resident throughout the year.

Waves of invaders
In the northwest, Alaska and Siberia have been joined at various times in the past when sea levels have lowered sufficiently to expose the bed of the shallow Bering Straight.

At its narrowest it is only 56 miles (90 km) across and no more than 150 ft (45 m) deep, so this land bridge has allowed newly evolved Eurasian species to cross over onto the American continent from time to time. On each occasion, the continent's existing fauna has been pushed southwards. Even now, traveling north to south provides a journey back through time as species of increasing antiquity are encountered along the way.

The animals of the far north clearly show their recent Eurasian origins. Species like the caribou (or reindeer as they are called in Europe), the wapiti or elk (Europe's red deer), moose, beavers and polar bears occur throughout the northern hemisphere. Other species like the grizzly bear and bison that occur further south have closely related European equivalents (the brown bear and the wissent), while lynxes, marmots, wolves and sheep are widely distributed groups with species on both sides of the Atlantic.

Southern evolution
As successive waves of immigrants made their way southwards, they naturally underwent further evolution away from their ancestral forms to develop adaptations to the new habitats in which they found themselves. Among these American-evolved species that occur further to the south are the pocket gophers, musk rats and prairie dogs, raccoons and skunks and several large mammals like the Rocky Mountain goat and the pronghorn antelope.

Birds, too, show similar relationships with the European species. Among the more characteristically American species, however, are the turkeys, sage grouse and road runners.

Alligator swamps
A belt of low-lying coastal plain occupies North America's southern margin, sweeping in a great S-shaped curve around the Gulf of Mexico and up the Atlantic seaboard as far as the Hudson River. It is an area of rich alluvial soils and inundated swamps, the most famous of which are the Florida Everglades.

The Everglades extend for about 100 miles (160 km) and occupy virtually the whole of the southern end of the Florida peninsula. They lie in a shallow basin formed by rising land around the coastal margins. The land is so flat that a rise of 2 ft (60 cm) in the water level would result in the flooding of hundreds of square miles of surrounding countryside.

The Everglades themselves are characterized by plains of sawgrass, a member of the sedge family that grows to heights of 15 ft (5 m). Around the edges, they merge into sand prairies, pineland, mangrove swamp and an area known as the Big Cypress Swamp consisting largely of gigantic swamp-cypresses.

These massive trees throw up knobbly pinnacles of wood from their roots through which they breathe air in order to gain the vital oxygen that is lacking from the dark swamp waters. These aerial roots provide a haven in which alligators lurk, watching for prey.

Earth's oldest plants
To the west of the Rocky Mountains, a smaller chain of mountains runs parallel to the coast. Between the Sierra Nevada section of this coastal range and the Rockies lies a roughly triangular area 800 miles (1290 km) long by 500 miles (800 km) wide at its northern end.

Known as the Great Basin, this area is thought to be the remains of a giant volcanic crater, with parts of its floor lying below sea level – the bottom of Death Valley is 282 ft (86 m) below the sea – and saline lakes like the Great Salt Lake of Utah and the Salton Sea in southern California are common. Elsewhere, much of the land is now desert, and in places the rock is a rich, deep red.

Tree-form cacti and thickets of silvery bitter-smelling sage-brush are characteristic of wilderness areas like the Mojave and Colorado deserts. Time moves slowly here: the agave or yucca produce their 12 ft (3.7 m) flower spikes only twice in a century, while creasote bushes – the oldest plants on earth with an age of several thousand years – grow by infinitesimal amounts in a human lifetime.

NORTH
POLE

ARCTIC

OCEAN

BERING

SEA

BEAUFORT

SEA

BAFFIN BAY

Arctic Circle

Mt McKinley
20,320 ft

Mackenzie

LABRADOR

SEA

HUDSON

BAY

Mt Rainier
14,408 ft

GREAT
LAKES

St Lawrence

Mt St Helens
9677 ft

Bad
Lands

Appalachian Mts

Hudson

NORTH

ATLANTIC

OCEAN

Mt Shasta
14,162 ft

GREAT
BASIN

Great
Salt
Lake

Sierra Nevada

San Andreas Fault

Death
Valley

Colorado

Grand
Canyon

Mississippi

Grande

GULF OF

MEXICO

Florida
Everglades

Tropic of Cancer

West
Indies

PACIFIC

OCEAN

Mt Popocatepetl
17,887 ft

CARIBBEAN SEA

Equator

| 0 | 200 | 400 | 600 | 800 | 1000 miles |
| 0 | 400 | 800 | 1200 | | 1600 km |

Coasts and Rivers

Right *America's northern coasts are often heavily indented with bays and creeks. Here, on the rugged coast of Newfoundland, stormy Atlantic waves are broken and reduced to fine spray and foam when they smash onto the jagged rocks.*

Far right *The sight of a humpback whale leaping out of the water is one of the most exhilarating sights of nature. The whales migrate up into the Arctic waters during the summer, and swim down into the warmer waters off Central America during the winter.*

Humpback whales are a highly social species, communicating with each other over vast distances by the means of very low haunting "songs".

Below *Dolphins are probably the most intelligent of the animal species. These agile sea mammals possess an unusually sophisticated natural language of clicks, whines, moans and whistles with which they communicate among themselves. Dolphins use echo-location — a form of sonar — to find the schools of fish on which they feed.*

Main picture *The Pacific coast contains spectacular sandy beaches that often lie at the foot of coastal mountain ranges running parallel to the continent's western seaboard. This Californian beach is about to be engulfed by a sudden blanket of impenetrable fog.*

Below left *The ghost crab's eye stalks seem to glow with an eerie light as it pauses to investigate an unfamiliar object while scuttling across a beach under cover of night.*

Below *On the Canadian border, Washington State's Olympic peninsula is dominated by the snow-capped mountains that give it its name. Descending right down to the coast, they continue into the water to form giant sea stacks.*

Above *The California sea otter has learned how to handle the poisonous spines of the sea urchin so that it can get at the flesh: it breaks off the spines by wrapping the sea urchin in a sheet of leathery kelp seaweed. It can also break open clam shells by smashing them against rocks held on the chest.*

Right *Salmon are spawned in the headwaters of the large rivers that empty into the Pacific and Atlantic coasts. After swimming downstream they spend as much as four years out at sea. Then they* return to breed in the headwaters of the streams in which they hatched. They find their way back largely by taste, being able to identify the characteristic scents of individual rivers even far out at sea. Once they have spawned, most then die.

Far right *The grizzly bear, largest of the land carnivores, can weigh as much as 900 lbs (400 kg). Like most bears, it is omnivorous and will eat anything from plants to bison. On the Pacific coast they have become very skilled at catching salmon swimming up the rivers to spawn.*

Alaska

Left *Mt McKinley's snow-bound summit rises to a height of 20 320 ft (6194 m), making it the highest mountain on the North American continent. This massive mountain's glaciers and icefields provide a dramatic backdrop to the Alaskan landscape. Its summit offers an unparalleled view for more than 100 miles (160 km) distance. Mt McKinley rises higher above the land on which it stands than any other mountain.*

Below *Walruses are related to seals, but are instantly recognized by their bristled moustaches and tusks, and usually grow to a length of 12 ft (3 m). The tusks of large individuals can grow to 2 ft (60 cm) in length. They are normally used to prize molluscs loose from the sea bed, but can serve as lethal weapons against enemies when required. Walruses live in small groups in the waters along the edge of the Arctic.*

Above *Great herds of caribou still roam the northern wastelands. They move up into the Arctic tundra during the summer; as winter closes in they retreat southwards before the advancing snows.*

Right *Like all deer, caribou males grow their antlers anew each spring. Initially these are covered in a soft sheath known as "velvet", but this has to be rubbed off before the antlers can harden into effective weapons. The size of a male's antlers is determined by his condition rather than his age.*

Far right *During the breeding season the males spar for the privilege of mating the females as they come on heat. Only the heaviest males with the biggest antlers will succeed.*

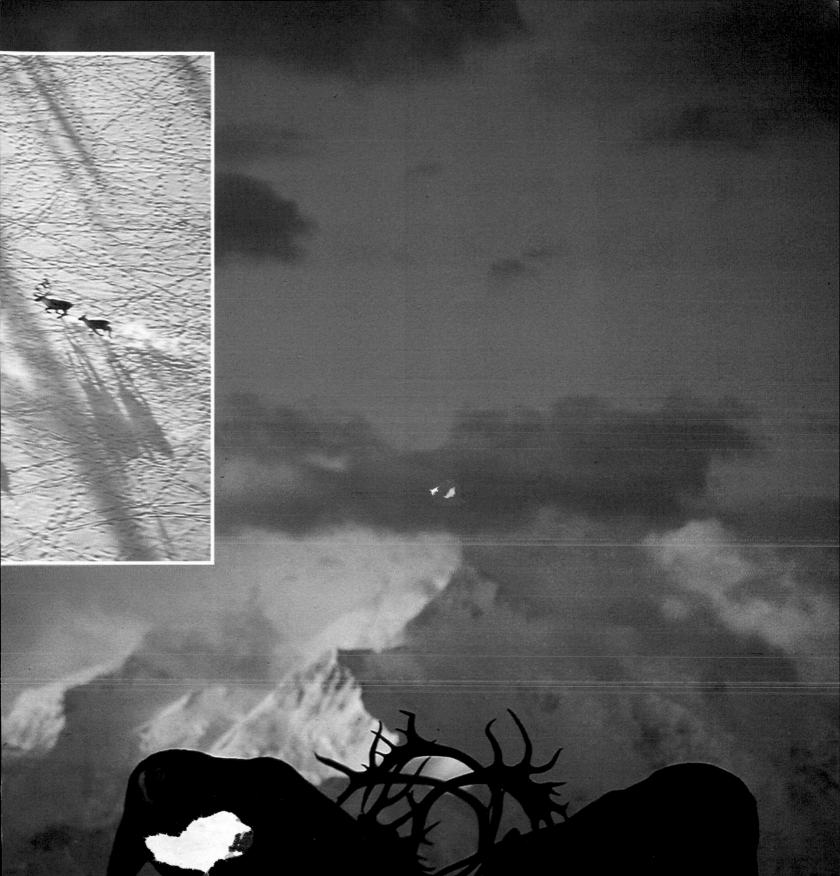

The Rockies

Left *The Rocky Mountains run the length of the continent, forming a barrier between the western coastal areas and the great plains to the east. These giant saw-toothed mountains raise their bare crests above the tree line.*

Below *Bighorn sheep roam the meadows and high pastures of the Rockies. During the breeding season the males use their massive horns as battering rams in head-shattering contests that often leave the combatants dazed and barely conscious.*

Bottom *The timber wolf is an accomplished hunter that lives in family groups. Its ability to cooperate in hunting and bringing down prey allows the wolf to take on larger animals like caribou and moose that are many times its own size.*

Above *An adult beaver eats willow branches while a juvenile looks on. Beavers build dams out of trees, stones and mud to create ponds so deep that the water does not freeze in winter. In the center of the dams they construct lodges with underwater entrances out of the same materials, where the family lives safe from predators throughout the year.*

Left *The bobcat or bay lynx is still common in the remote forests of the Rocky Mountains, where it preys on birds and small mammals. This one has caught a cottontail rabbit.*

Far left *The Yellowstone River plunging spectacularly over the 312 ft (96 m) Lower Falls into a deep canyon carved out of the heavily wooded Rocky Mountains. The Yellowstone National Park became the first national park in the world when it was established in 1872.*

93

REDWOODS

Redwoods and bigtrees, the two species of giant conifers that occur in the coastal mountains of California and Oregon, are among the largest and oldest living things on earth.

The redwood is found throughout the area and grows to immense heights with tall straight trunks. The tallest tree ever measured had a crown height of 364 ft (112 m).

The bigtrees of the Sierra Nevada Mountains in California are very much more massive, though not as tall as the redwoods. The largest bigtree specimen is the famous "General Sherman" in the Sequoia National Park. Although it stands at a mere 272 ft (83 m) in height, its circumference at ground level is over 100 ft (30 m). Its largest branch, 130 ft (40 m) above the ground, has a diameter in excess of 6 ft (2 m). The tree's total weight is estimated to be over 2150 tons (2 million kg), making it the largest living thing in the world. It carries 155 tons of foliage alone.

The trees take about 400 years to grow from seedlings into mature adults. Some of the bigtrees have been estimated to be more than 3000 years old after counts have been made of the concentric rings in their trunks. This means that they were already fully grown when Homer sat down to write the Iliad in ancient Greece.

The size and strength of the redwoods made them an early target for the lumberjacks after their discovery in the 1850s. As a result, many of the more accessible groves were destroyed before legislation could be passed to protect them. There are now only about 70 groves of bigtree sequoias in existence, mostly within the Sequoia National Park, which was first established in 1890 as a part of the Yosemite National Park.

Below *North Dome and Half Dome, Yosemite National Park.*

Right *General Sherman tree, Sequoia National Park.*

Left *The Least chipmunk is one of a number of species of these small ground squirrels that are widely distributed in the forests and mountains of North America. They live in burrows that they make themselves and spend some of the winter in partial hibernation. Chipmunks are almost entirely vegetarian, living off seeds and nuts, some of which are stored for the winter.*

Below *The Baltimore oriole, known for the rich warmth of its colors, is a member of a widespread group of American birds.*

The Bad Lands

Far to the north of the Grand Canyon lies another area of natural sculptures, the Bad Lands of Dakota.

Although their gullies and pillars are small by comparison with those of the Grand Canyon, the Bad Lands are famed for the unusual shapes produced by the rivers that eroded them out of the surrounding landscape.

The whole area is arid and inhospitable, orginally carved out by rivers flowing down from areas of heavy rainfall on their way to the great Missouri River to the east. Almost devoid of vegetation, the area was given the name Maka Sicha ("bad lands") by the local Dakota Indians long before the Europeans arrived.

Above *The extraordinary moonscapes of the Dakota Bad Lands owe their origins as much to the lack of vegetation as to the rivers that have washed away the fragile earth.*

Right *The rattlesnake uses the rattle at the end of its tail to warn off intruders. Provoked by too close an approach this western diamondback strikes, the fangs in its upper jaw extended to deliver a lethal dose of venom.*

Top right *Bands of wild horses, the descendants of animals brought over by the early colonists, roam the prairies of the Great Plains. In fights stallions use hooves and teeth to gain control over the herds of females.*

Main picture *The wooded savanna grasslands of South Dakota experience extremes of climate. Heavy winter snowfalls and hot dry summers combine to create conditions which few plants can tolerate.*

Top right *A wild turkey tom struts on his stamping ground during the breeding season. Turkeys were partially domesticated by the Indians long before the Europeans arrived. Within a century of the arrival of Columbus, however, they had been introduced into Europe where they soon became widespread as a domestic species.*

Below *The oppossum is the only marsupial (pouched) mammal to occur on the North American continent. It remained behind in forested areas long after the original primitive mammals that first colonized the continent had been forced southwards by the more highly evolved placental mammals arriving from Asia across the Alaskan peninsula.*

THE GRAND CANYON

A central strip of arid land weaves its way from the Dakotas in the north through into Mexico. The vegetation is often sparse and the soil sandy, owing to the low rainfall. Erosion caused by rivers flowing through from regions of higher rainfall elsewhere has frequently created landscapes of quite dramatic proportions. The most famous of these areas is Arizona's Grand Canyon, the largest natural chasm in the world. Formed by the River Colorado and its tributaries, the canyon's span varies from four to eighteen miles over its 270 mile (435 km) length, and in some parts is just over a mile (1.6 km) deep.

The Grand Canyon is a very recent feature on the geological time scale as it is barely more than one million years old, but it cuts down through *two billion* years of the earth's history compacted in the rocks and sandstones of the crust. The canyon is an extraordinary window on the past, providing us with tantalizing glimpses of the plant and animal life that once abounded and is now preserved as fossils in the rock.

Mountains and plateaus support luxuriant forests of juniper and piñon pines along the higher northern rim, with vanilla-scented yellow pines further up. The trees are snow-bound during winter, in striking contrast to the canyon's floor only a few miles away where desert conditions prevail. The forests of the plateaus abound with mule deer and prairie dogs that are hunted by cougars, bobcats and coyotes; but the canyon floor is too arid for anything except the gila monster, one of only two poisonous lizards in the world.

Further north in Utah the upper reaches of the Colorado river have created natural sculptures that are often exquisitely beautiful. Arched bridges of rock span the rivers, while slender pillars and outcrops litter the floors of the sheer-sided canyons.

Above *A cougar or mountain lion stalking a deer.*

Bottom *Monument Valley, Utah, is renowned for its natural sculptures.*

Right *The Grand Canyon cuts down through two billion years of fossilized history.*

Below *Bryce Canyon, Utah.*

Lightning is one of the most
spectacular sights of nature.
It is a discharge of electricity,
accompanied by a visible flash,
between two clouds or a cloud
and the earth. This flash of forked
lightning was photographed in
New Mexico during a dry
electrical storm.

Deserts

Above *The saguaro or tree cactus can grow to 70 ft (20 m) in height, with its candelabra branches dominating the scrub vegetation of the southwestern deserts. Near the tops of the branches it bears white flowers which later produce edible crimson fruits.*

Right *The peccary is a primitive member of the pig family. It lives in small bands of about 10 animals in the dry deserts and woodlands of the southern United States and South America. A very aggressive and sometimes dangerous animal, it is one of the few species to have successfully managed to invade the northern continent since the Central American landbridge linked North and South America.*

Far right *The yucca is a giant member of the lily family, and is one of the commonest plants in the Southern deserts. Some species have been known to grow to heights of 40 ft (12 m).*

Yuccas have a remarkable relationship with certain species of moths called yucca-moths. The moth takes balls of pollen collected from one flower to another plant where it lays four or five eggs along with the pollen balls.

The larvae, when they emerge, feed on the seeds produced by the fertilized flower. One larva needs about 20 seeds to complete its development, which leaves over 100 seeds for the plant to reproduce from. Each of the 30 species of yucca has its own species of moth, without which it cannot be fertilized.

Death Valley

Right *The floor of Death Valley is the lowest point on the continent at 282 ft (86 m) below sea level, and is renowned for its suffocating heat. No more than 50 miles (80 km) long and 20 miles (30 km) wide, it is surrounded by high mountains, many of which are snow-bound during winter.*

The Armagossa River flows into Death Valley from the south through a deep canyon. Unable to escape, its waters evaporate in temperatures that often exceed 120°F (49°C), leaving behind vast deposits of minerals and salt.

From Dantes View, at an altitude of 5475 ft (1669 m), you can look out over the white salt desert of Death Valley towards the snow-capped Panamint Mountains to the west.

Far right *Easily identified by the hour-glass marking on its abdomen, the female black widow is the most poisonous of all the spiders. Like all spiders the female usually kills and eats the smaller male after mating. The bite is even lethal to man.*

Below *The Mexican red-knee tarantula is one of a number of large spiders found throughout Central America and down into the neighboring southern continent. They occasionally catch animals as big as small birds by lying in wait in holes in the ground.*

The Everglades

Left *The coastal margins of the south and east contain innumerable swamps, large and small. The most famous of these are the Florida Everglades, a vast area of low-lying cypress and reed swamp. The dampness and the heat combine to produce a miasma that enhances the ghostly appearance of the trees, here festooned with strands of Spanish moss.*

Below left *The most infamous inhabitant of the swamps is the alligator. These carnivorous reptiles lurk among the tree roots and reeds, and prey on whatever comes their way.*

Below *Alligators are conscientious parents, attentively guarding their clutch of eggs and tolerantly looking after the young after they have hatched.*

Above *Roseate spoonbills are one of the most characteristic species of birds in the waterlogged swamps of the southeast. They use their long spade-like bills to sift small animals from the muddy bottom of the swamps. These beautiful birds were once almost exterminated by hunters collecting their delicately shaded feathers.*

Far left *The mangrove is adapted to a life with its base permanently submerged in water. It is a very hardy tree sending out roots from the trunk that spread outwards to sprout into new trees.*

Left *An anhinga dries its wings in the sun. This large diving bird uses its long pointed beak to spear fish while swimming underwater.*

South America

outh America stretches across the equator and reaches as far south as the turbulent waters of the Antarctic. It is a continent of extremes including the torrid swamps of its Caribbean coast, storm-tossed islands at its southern tip, dense tropical forests, vast arid grasslands, towering mountains with high, icy uninhabited wildernesses. The continent includes the world's driest desert, its largest river and most extensive area of rainforest. There are still great tracts of land untouched by modern civilizations, but the rate of destruction of many habitats is accelerating and unique communities of plants and animals are disappearing every day.

Mountains of the Incas

The Andes form one of the largest mountain systems in the world, running for more than 5000 miles (8000 km) from the Cordillera Mountains of Colombia and western Venezuela in the north, to the peaks of the Chilean Andes at the continent's southernmost tip. In average height, the Andes are exceeded only by the Himalayas. Although the Andes are not simply a continuation of the North American Rocky Mountains system, they were formed in much the same way – through the impact of the westward-drifting South American continent with the submerged floor of the southern Pacific Ocean.

In northern Chile this great mountain chain narrows down to a double row of peaks, many of which exceed 20 000 ft (6100 m) in altitude. Between the peaks, steep passes and high valleys lie at altitudes of more than 10 000 ft (3050 m), too cold and dry to produce anything but near-desert. Herds of guanacos graze on the impoverished grasslands, preyed on by mountain lion (puma) and wolves.

To the north and south, the Andes are both lower and wider, often being broken up, as in Colombia, into a series of parallel ranges. In Peru, the mountains form a broad high-altitude plateau at 13 000 to 15 000 ft (3960 to 4570 m).

Life below the snow line

On the vast windswept moorlands, the guanaco's smaller, fine-fleeced relative, the vicuna, ranges below the snow line, while chinchillas, rabbit-sized rodents with thick, soft gray fur, scurry about among the frost-shattered rocks. Above them, the giant Andean condor soars among the peaks, covering hundreds of miles in its perpetual search for carrion.

Lower down, among the forests of the northwest Andes lives the spectacled

Guanacos live high up in the cold wastes of the Andes. They are related to camels and have only two toes on each foot.

bear, the only bear to be found in the southern hemisphere, as well as the tusked Andean deer and the delicate pudu, the smallest deer in the New World, standing just 13 in (33 cm) high.

400-year drought
The continent's western coast, hemmed in by the peaks of the Andes, is very narrow. In Chile, a line of coastal mountains runs parallel to the Andes, forming steep escarpments that drop 2000 ft (600 m) straight into the sea. Inland, behind this range of hills, lies the Atacama desert. It claims the longest drought on record: no rain has fallen here for over 400 years.

Further to the south the coast breaks up into a complex of largely deserted islands that culminate in the continent's sub-antarctic tip, the icy but beautiful islands of Tierra del Fuego. These rugged islands lie in the path of the "Roaring Forties", winds of hurricane speed which whip up violent storms between Tierra del Fuego and the Antarctic peninsula.

Primeval rainforest
The Amazon basin is in the heart of the South American continent, an endless tract of primeval tropical rainforest covering some two million square miles (5.2 million sq km). The river is by far the largest in the world in terms of volume of water, with an average width of about five miles (8 km) and depth of over 100 ft (30 m).

However, the Amazon often divides into two or more channels, themselves full of islands, large and small. In its lower reaches, the river broadens to a width of 40 miles (65 km) while at its outlet on the Atlantic coast it is more than 100 miles (160 km) across.

Although the Amazon rises on the slopes of the Andes, only a few hundred miles from the Pacific Ocean, it travels thousands of miles eastwards to the Atlantic, through a massive flat-bottomed basin. Because of the shallowness of the basin's profile, the river winds a convoluted course through the rainforest, and 11 of its tributaries flow for more than 1000 miles (1610 km) without a single waterfall or set of rapids.

"Black" and "white" rivers
Rivers like the Negro that originate on these jungle soils carry no nutrients at all and are known as "black water" rivers, though usually more the color of strong tea. They contain many toxic chemicals derived from the plants that rot on their banks or fall into them, and as a result are virtually devoid of life. But rivers that originate on the soils of the Andes, like the Amazon itself, are often heavily laden with rich silt. Known as "white water" rivers from their light coffee color, they deposit desperately needed nutrients on the forest floor during their annual floods.

The Amazon forest is remarkable for its variety of species, showing a diversity that far exceeds anything ever seen in temperate forests. Instead of a few kinds of tree dominating the jungle, there are dozens of different species, some reaching high up in the thick forest canopy, others occupying the middle or lower storeys.

Nuts and purple-hearts
Trees like the Brazil nut, cream nut, virola and purple-heart grow to enormous heights, many propped up by massive buttress roots, while valuable trees such as mahogany, rosewood and snakewood are found in the lower storey, together with palm species in a variety and profusion unrivalled anywhere else in the world. Clustered on the trees are masses of perching orchids, ferns, cacti, tradescantia and bromeliads.

On the lower slopes of the Andes, ivory nut palm and passion flower become increasingly common, along with bignoniad vines and calliandras with their brilliant red cockades at flowering time. This forest has produced more plants of economic value than any other. From deep within it have come the plants that give us rubber, quinine and cocaine, as well as cassava, guava, calabash, pineapples and, probably, the tomato.

Despite the luxuriance of plant life, the forest is relatively thinly populated with mammals. The most abundant inhabitants are monkeys; marmosets, titis, sakis, squirrel monkeys and the scarlet-faced uakari. Howler monkeys boom through the forests with their resonating morning calls, while sloths work their way methodically through their upside-down world. Tree-dwelling anteaters, porcupines, opossums, coatis, kinkajous, ocelots, jaguarundis and jaguars occur widely throughout the area, though nowhere in large numbers.

The fight to survive
In the deep shade of the forest floor, few large animals disturb the stillness, but in the clearings and along the riverbanks, marsh deer, tapir, giant anteaters and herds of pig-like peccaries search for food. At night, they themselves are the victims of vampire bats. Coypu and capybara – at 3 ft (90 cm) long, the largest rodent in the world – live along the water's edge, while alligators, pirhana fish, boa constrictors and anacondas lurk in the rivers.

In and above the forest canopy, where the dense foliage knits together to form a continuous layer far above the ground, there is a stunning variety of bird and insect life. During the day, the forests ring with the raucous cries of parrots, parakeets, macaws and toucans, while at night they echo to the calls of nightjars and whip-poor-wills, mingled with the metallic whirring of insects.

Giant beetles
The forests are literally alive with insects. The Goliath beetle, Titanus, with a body length of 6 in (15 cm), is the largest beetle in the world. Butterflies and moths are everywhere: 700 species were once collected from a single place – more than double the number of species that occur in the whole of Europe.

The Amazon is renowned for its fantastic variety of frogs which come in every size, shape, color and voice imaginable. Highly poisonous species breed in lagoons, pools and even in the rainwater collected by plants. They are distinguished by their bright colors. One species is used by the Amazonian Indians to produce an arrow poison so deadly that a few drops smeared on an arrowhead will kill a large monkey instantly, and a man within minutes.

Gigantic waterfalls
To the north and south of the Amazon basin lies the plateau of the Brazilian shield. The edges often form marked escarpments over which the rivers plunge in waterfalls that commonly exceed 1000 ft (305 m) in height. The most dramatic of these is, without doubt, the remote Angel Falls on the Carrao River in southeastern Venezuela. With a drop of close to 3000 ft (915 m), these are the highest waterfalls in the world.

Swamps and pampas
To the south of the Brazilian highlands lie the lowland swamps of the River Plate and its three great tributaries, the Uruguay, the Paraná and the Paraguay. Here, running northwest for some 600 miles (965 km) is the Argentinian pampas. Pampas grass produces feathery 9 foot (3 m) seed spikes in the summer.

The central strip of the pampas is an almost level plain that rises imperceptibly as it runs north and west towards the Andes. Although much of this land is now used for agriculture, wild areas remain, where pampas cats and the long-legged maned wolf run down the pampas deer. To the north, the pampas give way to the Gran Chaco, an extensive area of marshes, lagoons and dense tropical jungle running northwards through Paraguay into one of the least explored areas on the continent, the Mato Grosso area of southwestern Brazil.

CARIBBEAN SEA

NORTH
ATLANTIC
OCEAN

Trinidad

Orinoco

Caroni

Guyana
Highlands

Galapagos
Islands

Mt Cotopaxi
19 344 ft

AMAZON

Negro

Amazon

Equator

Madeira

BASIN

A
N
D
E
S

Lake
Titicaca

Mato
Grosso

Brazilian Highlands

Atacama Desert

Grand
Chaco

Tropic of Capricorn

de la Plata

PACIFIC

OCEAN

Pampas

SOUTH
ATLANTIC
OCEAN

PATAGONIA

Falkland
Islands

Tierra
del
Fuego

| 0 | 200 | 400 | 600 | 800 | 1000 miles |

| 0 | 400 | 800 | 1200 | 1600 km |

The Andes

The Andes run the length of South America's west coast. This is the longest chain of mountains in the world, with many of the high valleys lying at great altitudes, and much of it a cold stony desert reaching up to the great jagged snow-capped peaks.

Right *In the cold dry air of the high Andean plateau, the ghostly gray shapes of the barrel cacti are one of the few signs of life.*

Below *A glistening blue and white glacier inches its way down a wide valley between craggy Andean peaks.*

The high peaks of the Andes provide ideal flying conditions for large birds. They rely on up-draughts created by the mountains to soar effortlessly on the thin air at 15 000 ft (4600 m) above sea level. These are just the sort of conditions that vultures like: from high above the land their sharp eyes can scan wide areas in search of carrion.

Right *The king vulture has few rivals for the title of ugliest bird on earth.*

Below *With a 9 ft (2.7 m) wingspan, the graceful Andean condor is the continent's largest bird. It lays its two large white eggs on inaccessible ledges on the mountain crags.*

Opposite *Against the background of the Andes' craggy peaks, small herds of guanacos roam the high altitude moorlands along the snow line, gleaning a precarious living from the sparse grasslands. A close relative of the camel, the guanaco can survive the intense cold of these windswept mountains only because its fine-fleeced coat keeps it warm.*

119

THE GALAPAGOS ISLANDS

The Galapagos archipelago consists of several hundred islands of all sizes, mostly of volcanic origin, that lie on the equator 650 miles (1050 km) west of the Ecuador coast. The islands are famous for the extent to which the few species that found their way there have diversified into many different forms, with each island often having its own race. It has usually been assumed that most species reached the archipelago by sea on floating vegetation from the South American continent, but it is possible that at some point the islands were connected by a landbridge to Central America, which would explain the close affinities between the respective wildlife species.

The name "Galapagos" derives from the Spanish word for tortoise, of which 15 species were once found on the islands. The most famous of these is the giant tortoise, which often grows to as much as 500 lbs (227 kg) in weight. Some individuals are known to have lived for more than 200 years, making them the longest lived animals on our planet.

Darwin's finches were one of the few groups of birds to reach the islands and their seed-eating ancestors gradually evolved into forms that occupied many of the niches filled by other bird families on the American mainland. Some evolved the thin beaks suitable for gleaning insects off leaves, others the thick heavy beaks characteristic of species that have to crack open hard nuts. The distances between the islands meant that each tended to evolve its own unique species to fill these ecological roles. Study of this diversity during a visit to the islands was a key factor that led nineteenth-century biologist Charles Darwin to develop his theory of evolution by natural selection.

Left *The Galapagos islands receive little rainfall and the vegetation is often sparse. Some islands have little to offer other than cacti, while much of the lower lying coastal areas are bare volcanic rock.*

Above left *A pair of Galapagos hawks squabble over a kill.*

Above center *Gargoyle-like iguanas live off algae growing in the sea.*

Above right *Frigate birds breed on many isolated oceanic islands, including the Galapagos.*

Below *South America has more spectacular waterfalls than any other continent. Deep in the impenetrable jungles of the interior, rivers plunge over the rims of steep-sided plateaus where the landscape has been eroded away to expose the underlying layers of hard rock. Here the River Iguacu pours over wide horseshoe-shaped falls in Southern Brazil.*

Right *The Tillandsia is a relative of the domesticated pineapple, and is one of many species of bromeliads that perch on other trees. They obtain their nutrients by tapping into the host plant or directly from the atmosphere.*

Far right *With a free fall of 3000 ft (915 m), Venezuela's Angel Falls are the highest in the world. The Carrao River pours off the edge of the high plateau and is transformed into little more than spray by the time it reaches the riverbed at the base of the cliff.*

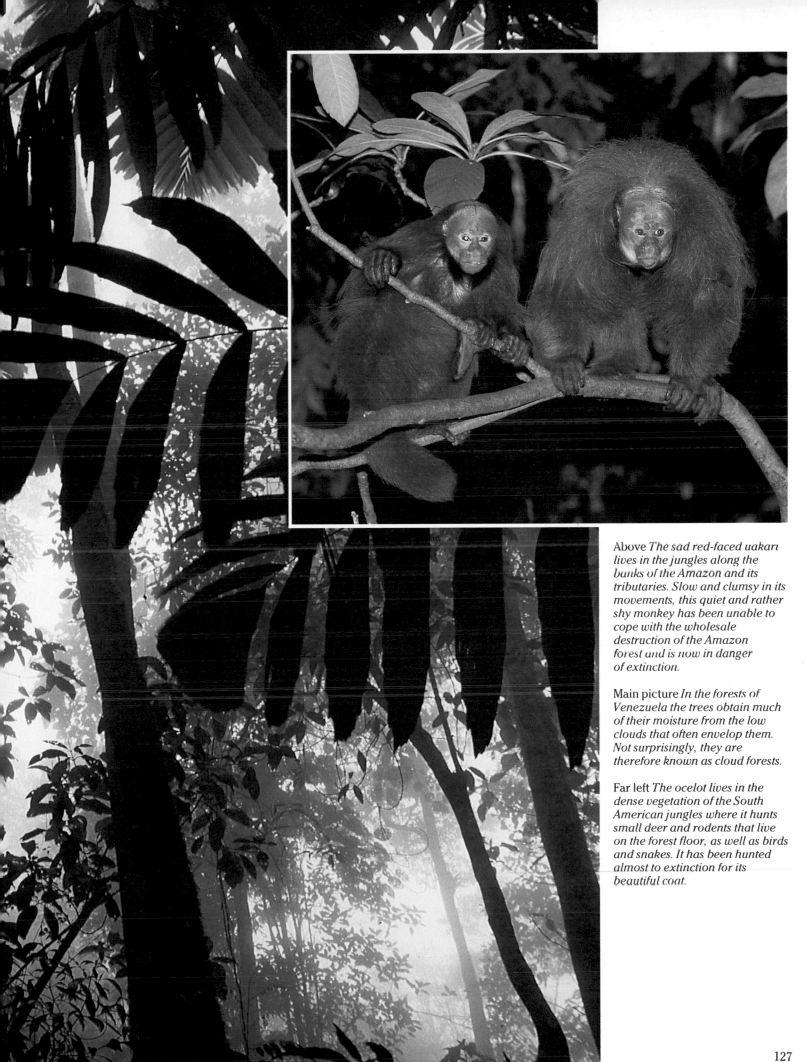

Above *The sad red-faced uakari lives in the jungles along the banks of the Amazon and its tributaries. Slow and clumsy in its movements, this quiet and rather shy monkey has been unable to cope with the wholesale destruction of the Amazon forest and is now in danger of extinction.*

Main picture *In the forests of Venezuela the trees obtain much of their moisture from the low clouds that often envelop them. Not surprisingly, they are therefore known as cloud forests.*

Far left *The ocelot lives in the dense vegetation of the South American jungles where it hunts small deer and rodents that live on the forest floor, as well as birds and snakes. It has been hunted almost to extinction for its beautiful coat.*

127

The Amazon Basin

Below *There are several species of vampire bats, all of which live on blood. Shunning even moonlight, they leave their roosts in search of victims only on dark nights. Flying just a few feet above the ground, they locate their victims by echo-location. They land just a few yards away and walk over to the prey using the "wrists" of their wings for support.*

Right *Contrary to popular myth, vampire bats do not use fangs to suck blood from their victims. Rather, they use their razor-sharp incisor teeth to gouge out a small slice of skin, then they lick the blood that oozes out of the wound. Their saliva contains a chemical that prevents the blood clotting and keeps the wound open. After spending up to 15 minutes on a victim, the bat will have ingested more than its own body weight in blood. Until some of the liquid has been excreted, the bat is barely able to fly.*

Right *The jaguarundi is one of the least cat-like of the cat family, and is sometimes known as the "otter-cat". It is an accomplished swimmer, equally at home in the water or climbing trees. It lives on the many small mammals and birds that abound in the forests of the Amazon and Orinoco basins. The jaguarundi is a solitary animal, active both during the day and at night.*

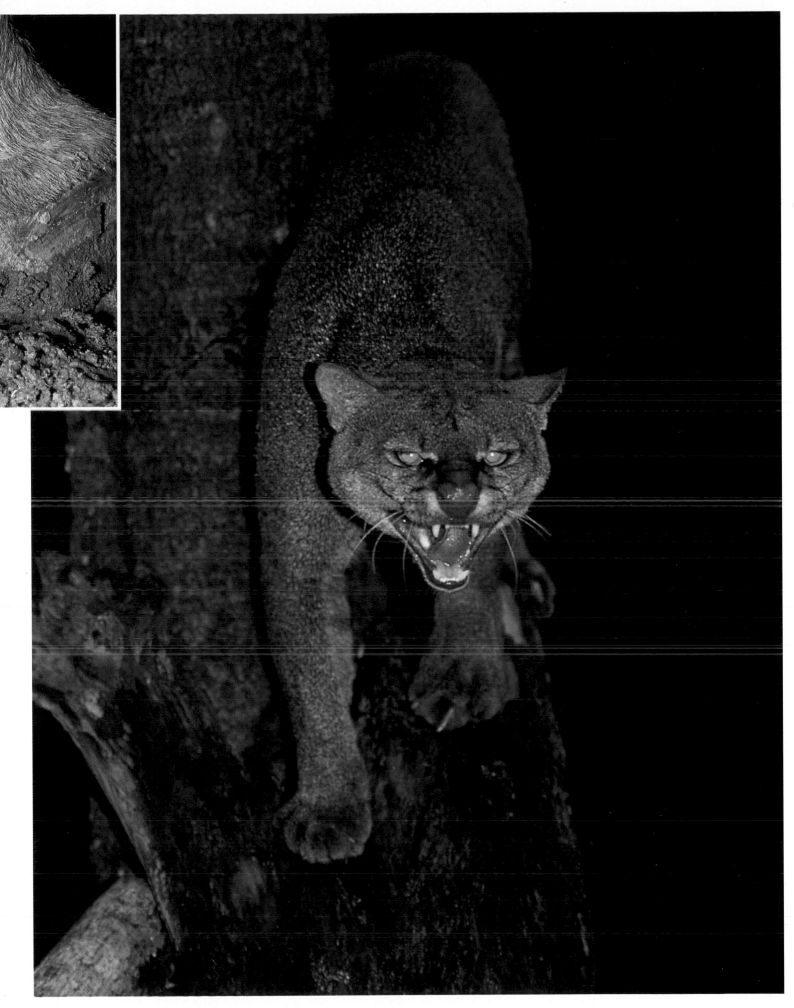

Top left *Boa constrictors do not have poison glands or fangs, so kill their prey — usually small birds or mammals — by squeezing it to death. Boa constrictors are excellent climbers, and prefer the open forest along river banks.*

Left *The jaguar is the largest of the cat family on either of the American continents, and sadly is now very rare. It preys on deer, rodents and peccaries for which it lies in wait on the forest floor. An excellent swimmer, it sometimes even catches crocodiles and fish in the rivers.*

Above *The northeastern coasts of South America consist of a maze of murky swamps and forest. The creeks teem with alligators, fish and brightly colored waterbirds.*

Macaws, large colorful members of the parrot family, are among the most characteristic sights of the South American forests. They live in noisy groups, their shrill raucous cries ringing through the trees as they flit across sun-lit glades.

The name "macaw" comes from the fact that they often eat the violet scented oil-nuts of the macaw palm using their massive bills to crack open the nuts. In this picture, scarlet macaws and red-and-green macaws mingle peacefully on a cliff face in Peru.

Left *The axolotl has smooth skin and feathery external gills and looks like something from outer space. In fact it is the larval stage of the Mexican tiger salamander which is inhibited by cold temperatures at high altitudes from undergoing metamorphosis into the adult form. Instead, it retains its larval appearance even though it still becomes sexually mature.*

Many frogs in the forests of Central and South America produce an especially toxic poison from the glands in their skin, intended to discourage predators from eating them. These poisons were used by native Indians to tip arrow-heads, hence their name of arrow-poison frog.

The bright colors of an arrow-poison frog from Guyana (left) and a red-and-green arrow-poison frog from the rainforests of Costa Rica (below) warn predators that these potential meals are extremely poisonous and best left alone.

HUMMINGBIRDS

Hummingbirds are related to the swifts, but, unlike swifts, are renowned for their irridescent colors and ability to hover in flight while collecting nectar from flowers. They range in size from the 8 inch (20 cm) long *Patagona* hummingbird of the Andes down to the tiny fairy hummingbird of Cuba which has a body length of less than 2 in (5 cm) and a weight of under 2 g.

Their narrow beaks enable them to get down into the flower tubes of certain plants where they use their unusually long thin tongues to probe for nectar and insects while hovering in mid-air.

They have had to evolve the ability to fly backwards in order to be able to extricate themselves from the flowers when they want to fly off. The wingbeat is so rapid that it creates an audible hum as the bird flies, hence their name. In some of the smaller species, the beat is so fast that the wings are lost in a blur.

Far left *A female blue-tailed woodstar hummingbird feeds her chicks in the nest. Most species of hummingbird build a tiny cup nest out of vegetable down, plant fibers and spider webs.*

Left *A rufous-breasted hermit hummingbird hovers in front of a hibiscus flower and pushes its beak up into the nectar pool at the base of the flower tube.*

Below *A male broadbilled hummingbird works its beak in between the petals of a flower. Hummingbirds have greatly enlarged breastbones and flying muscles to provide them with the power and fine control needed for precision flying.*

The Pampas

Below *The feathery heads of pampas grass grow to heights of 8 ft (2.5 m) on the flat plains of the Argentinian Pampas. They create an illusion of rippling water as they shimmer in the breeze.*

Bottom *In the grasslands of the Mato Grosso a giant anteater prepares to tackle a termite mound. This toothless mammal uses its powerful claws to break open the concrete-like nest so that it can get at the termites inside with its long sticky tongue.*

Left *The arid plains of Patagonia stretch for 1000 miles (1600 km) down into the southern tip of South America. It is a vast empty landscape that varies from coarse grassland to stony desert. The plain fills the space between the Atlantic and the foothills of the Andes on the western side of the continent.*

Since there is very little rainfall here only a small handful of the rivers that flow eastwards from the snow-capped Andes contain water all year round and many of the lakes that occupy depressions in the plateau are saline. Nonetheless, Patagonia is surprisingly rich in wildlife. Herds of guanacos range on the grasslands along the Andean foothills. The mara or Patagonian cavy is a graceful hare-like rodent that lives in burrows, as do many of the other rodent species that abound here. These provide ample food both for birds of prey and carnivores like the puma.

Inset left *The rhea is related to the ostrich and is native to South America. Outside the breeding season the birds gather in groups and take turns to keep watch for predators.*

139

SOUTH AMERICAN MAMMALS

As successive waves of newly evolved species invaded the American continent from Asia via the Alaskan landbridge, the native American species were pushed southwards. While their relatives further north died out, those in South America suffered less from the competition of the new Eurasian species and so survived. South America became an evolutionary dead-end where remnants of the more primitive species accumulated.

Among these were such primitive mammals as the opossums (the only marsupial or pouched mammal to occur outside Australia) and the edentates or "toothless mammals", which include the anteaters, sloths and armadillos.

The South American monkeys are also very different from those of the Old World. All have prehensile tails that can be used as a fifth hand by wrapping them around branches. Unlike the Old World monkeys, none of the New World species have adapted to life on the ground. As a result, they are all confined to the forests, where they are vulnerable to extinction as the trees are cut down around them.

Because groups like the antelopes, apes and horses evolved in the Old World long after South America's separation from Africa, none of these animals ever reached this continent. Consequently, the whole range of ecological niches occupied by these groups in the Old World remained unfilled in the New World. These included many open country habitats normally occupied by the grazing species. Other groups of mammals not normally associated with such habitats and lifestyles moved in to fill the vacant niches on the South American continent. These include the camel family, which originally evolved in North America but was pushed down into the southern continent by the Eurasian invaders from the north where they gave rise to the guanaco and the vicuna.

The most extraordinary development, however, took place among the rodents. These diversified so much that they filled many of the niches occupied by rabbits and antelopes in the Old World. They range from the small guinea pigs of the northeast to the tiny chinchillas of the high Andes and the hare-like maras of Patagonia.

Right *The armadillo is one of the most primitive of the placental mammals. When it curls up into a ball the armored plates on its back form an impregnable defence against most predators.*

Below left *Sloths spend most of their lives hanging upside down from branches suspended by their powerful hooked claws. Although almost helpless on the ground, they can swim quite well.*

Below right *The capybara is the largest rodent in the world. Living in dense forests along the edge of rivers and swamps it spends a good deal of its time in the water. Capybara live in groups of up to 20 individuals and are exclusively vegetarian.*

The Coastline

Left *Green turtles come ashore on the sandy beaches to lay their eggs. When the eggs hatch (below left) tiny turtles make their way in their thousands down the beach on the long journey out to the sea. Predatory seabirds ensure that few survive this ordeal.*

Below *In the warmer tropical waters of the Caribbean manatees graze the aquatic vegetation in the bays and estuaries around the coast. When not feeding, they rest on the sea bed.*

Far left *San Andreas gulls wade in the shallows on the Peruvian coast. South America's western coast is washed by the Humboldt current which brings cool water up from the Antarctic. It has an abundant supply of all types of fish which attract many sea birds that live on the seashore and nearby islands. The five and a half million birds that breed on just one tiny set of islands off the coast of Peru are said to consume more than 1000 tons (1 million kg) of fish a day.*

Far left *In northern Chile the mountains come right down to the coast where they form massive sea cliffs that are slowly being eaten away by wave erosion. The successive layers of sediment that were laid down year by year are clearly visible on the wind-polished cliffs.*

Left *A pair of Peruvian boobies guard their chicks.*

Left below *Tropic birds with their long forked tails are one of a group of sea birds capable of navigating the vast expanses of the world's oceans. This red-billed tropic bird skims the sea in search of fish off the continent's west coast.*

Asia

Asia is the largest continent on the planet, accounting for fully one-third of the earth's total land surface. Its most dramatic feature is, without question, the great Himalayan mountain chain. Forced upwards by the impact of the Indian sub-continent as it drifted northwards and collided with the Asian mainland, the high plateaus and peaks of the Himalayas form the roof of the world. The valleys of Tibet lie well above 12 000 ft (3600 m) and the high peaks that surround them tower a further 12 000 ft above that.

The frost line

Much of this world lies above the frost line, beyond which plant life cannot survive. In the snow deserts, the silence is broken only by the eerie howling of the winds in the ferocious winter storms. But on their margin, the moorlands are grazed by wild yak, largest of the cattle family, the bharal or blue sheep, and the chiru, a relative of the antelopes. They, in turn, are preyed on by the beautiful snow leopard, perhaps the most elusive of the big cats. In sheltered valleys, thickets of rhododendron are interspersed with grassy slopes that burst into flower in the spring time when blue poppies form bright carpets under the deep blood-red flowers of the poinsettia.

Bamboo forests

The lower slopes of the Himalayas are covered in dense forests. Native animals include the sambur and barasingha deer and Himalayan tahr, while in the rocky gullies live goat-antelopes like the serow and goral. The Himalayan forests are rich in bird life, notably hill mynahs and kingfishers, metallic-colored sunbirds and brilliantly plumed trogons. And the forest glades are filled with butterflies. By comparison, frogs, lizards and snakes are uncommon, even completely absent in the higher reaches of the mountains.

To the east lie the bamboo-forested mountains of Szechwan where the giant panda and its smaller relative, the red panda, feed exclusively on bamboo. Here, too, lives the takin, a distant relative of the musk ox. At lower altitudes, Chinese water deer with their tusked canine teeth and the raccoon dog (really a kind of fox) roam the forests. But, above all, this area is renowned for its pheasants, which come in almost every shape and color imaginable. Many are familiar as aviary birds in the west, and one has been spread worldwide as a gamebird.

Mount Fuji has the most perfect volcanic cone in the world. It is Japan's highest mountain at 12 385 (3775 m) and its beautifully symmetrical outline acts as a scenic backdrop for much of central Japan.

147

The high deserts of Asia

To the north of these mountain ranges, lying in a great swathe across the center of the continent, are the high deserts of central Asia. Stretching from Mongolia's great Gobi desert in the east, through Turkestan and the deserts of southern Russia to the Iranian plateau, it eventually passes into the lower lying deserts of the Arabian peninsula. The climate varies almost as much as the habitat, ranging from the winter snows of southern Mongolia to the dry heat of the Middle East. Bactrian camels and the kulan, a wild ass, graze the waterless thorn-scrub wastes of the Gobi, while in the west, ibex and markhor clamber among the rocky hills.

The Russian steppe

Stretching northwards to the Arctic Circle beyond these deserts lies the great Russian steppe, the largest plain in the world. Along the Arctic Circle are found the familiar species of the Scandinavian and American tundra – reindeer (caribou), musk ox, and lemmings – but it has its own specialties, too, like the curious little Siberian water shrew.

To the east, the plain rises into the Siberian taiga, a massive expanse of worn-down mountains that stretch from the Gobi desert north to the tundra plains on the Arctic Circle and east to the coastal plain on the north Pacific coast. This area of low, rolling mountains is all but continuous forest. On the lower-lying land in the north, it forms swamp forest, but this gives way to endless tracts of dark, gloomy coniferous forest on the higher ground.

Lake Baykal

Almost in the center of this area lies Lake Baykal, a long narrow freshwater lake with a total length of 420 miles (675 km). It is over 4500 ft (1370 m) deep in places, and the lake floor is more than 3000 ft (900 m) below sea level, making it the deepest lake in the world, as well as the one that penetrates furthest into the earth's crust.

Baykal is also one of the oldest lakes in the world, having been in existence for more than 140 million years. It is a museum of ancient species. The waters teem with fish, notably sturgeon and herring, and there is at least one species of fish whose nearest relatives are found only in the deepest parts of the oceans. The lake also has its own species of freshwater seal, apparently descended from animals that swam more than 2000 miles (3200 km) up the Yenisey and Angara rivers from the Arctic Ocean.

The southeastern corner of Asia is dominated by forests, ranging from the temperate forests of southern China to the tropical jungles of Borneo and the Indonesian islands. The whole area is much influenced by the ridges of hills that stand roughly northwest to southeast. Between them run the great rivers of the area, the Irrawaddy, the Salween, the Mekong and the Yangtze, all of which begin life in or near the Tibetan plateau.

The characteristic trees of the tropical forests are the Dipterocarps that push through the forest canopy to tower 200 ft (60 m) above the ground. Festooned with lianas and climbing figs, these giants provide pathways through the forest for a great many arboreal animals including several dozen species of macaque and langur monkeys. These forests are also home for gibbons and siamangs, the smallest of the apes, which move through the trees by swinging on their exceptionally long arms.

Dawn chorus

The early morning stillness is broken each day by the great calls of the gibbons staking their territorial claims. Replying in turn, the males of the family groups swing through the uppermost layers of the forest giving a prolonged series of whoops and booms. The calls rise to a crescendo of excitement and noise that passes in waves through the forest.

Among the lower storeys of the jungle, delicate large-eyed primates known as lorises climb with infinite care while giant squirrels, civets and the armor-plated pangolins scamper through the trees. On the forest floor, hare-sized mouse deer, tapirs and wild pigs provide rich pickings for the tiger and the clouded leopard. Other denizens of the forests include at least three species of wild cattle: the massive gaur, the miniature anoa barely larger than a sheep, and the wild Asiatic buffalo.

The wealth of fruiting trees, in particular the wild figs and the durian, attract a host of fruit-eating animals. Hornbills and pigeons gather around them, as well as the fruit-eating bats, the largest of their kind. With large night-seeing eyes and dog-like faces, these animals are very different from insect-eating bats, and their appearance has earned them the name of flying foxes.

Borneo

Around the southern coast of Indo-China lies a chain of islands, the projecting tips of a submerged continental shelf running out from the Indo-Chinese peninsula. Borneo is a typical member of this group of islands, but it also has some interesting features all of its own. Unlike most of its neighbors, it has no orderly chain of mountains running down its spine. Instead there is a confused jumble of mountains and rivers, all buried under the third largest tropical forest in the world. Many parts of the island have yet to be explored in any detail. Only Mt Kinabalu, the highest mountain in southeast Asia, rises above the tree line, its bare granite peak breaking through the overlying sandstones to reach an altitude of 13 430 ft (4094 m).

Mangroves and turtles

Around the coasts the shallow seas have led to the proliferation of mangrove forests. Just out from the shore lie the Turtle Islands, one of the last remaining breeding grounds of the edible turtle. The female turtles come ashore each year to lay upwards of two million eggs on a sandy beach that is no more than five acres (two hectares) in extent.

Giant dipterocarp trees and the aptly named ironwoods tower above a dense understorey of palms, ferns and rhododendrons. The rafflesia is the largest flower in the world with most of its bulk below ground. It smells of rotting flesh to attract the flies that pollinate it.

In the numerous pools, lotus flowers float upon the surface of the water. Orchids and other epiphytes of the most exotic kinds hang in the trees, while carnivorous pitcher plants have lethal traps for catching flying insects which are digested in a pool of juices.

Venomous ants

The jungles of Borneo are renowned for their insect life. Anyone daring to explore there will have to put up with sandflies, mosquitoes and flying insects. The local fire ants have some of the most venomous stings on earth. Other hazards include leeches, which crawl through the vegetation or swim in the rivers by the million, and pythons and king cobras, probably the most aggressive snakes in the world. These deadly reptiles wait in the undergrowth for unwary passers-by, while crocodiles lurk on the river banks.

But not all Borneo's forest life is so unpleasant. Its butterflies and moths are among the most beautiful in the world, and the giant Rajah Brooke's birdwing is probably the most outstanding butterfly on earth.

While many of the more conventional Asian mammals are found in these forests, the islands of the Malay archipelago also boast a number of their own specialties. The only great ape to be found in Asia, the orang-utan (Malay for "man of the forest"), threads its solitary way through the jungle. Tarsiers, the most primitive of all the primates, are thought to be rather like the original stock from which the primates, monkeys and apes, and man developed.

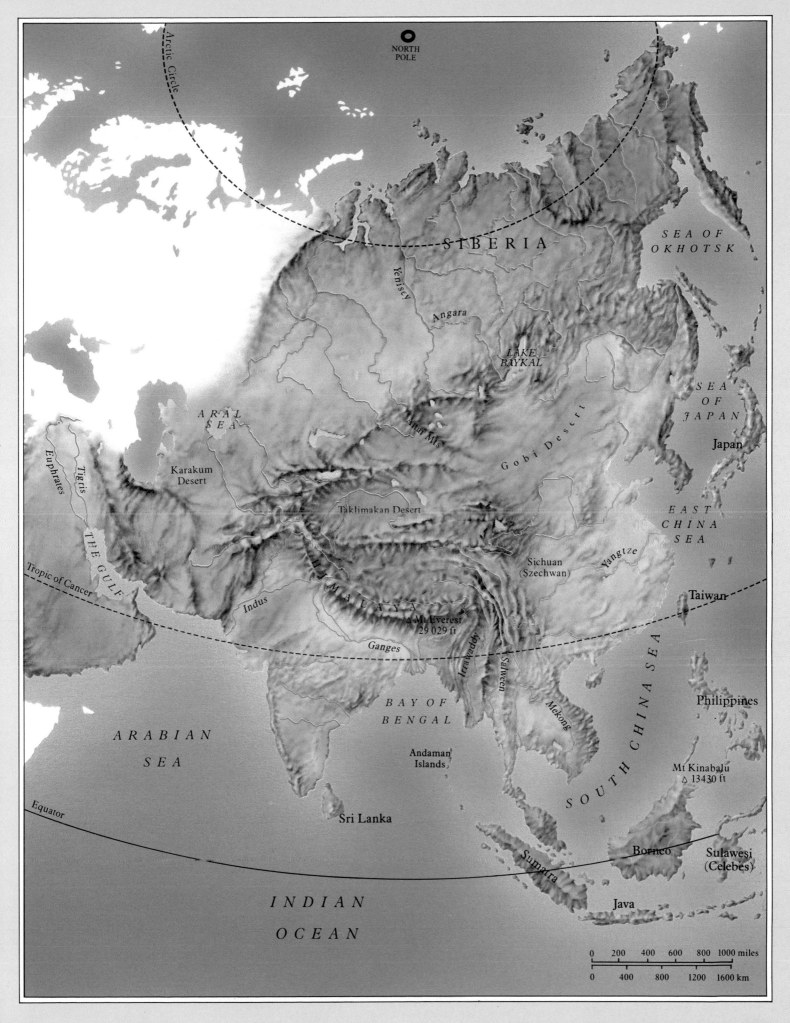

NORTH
POLE

Arctic Circle

SIBERIA

SEA OF
OKHOTSK

Yenisey

Angara

LAKE
BAYKAL

SEA
OF
JAPAN

Japan

ARAL
SEA

Altai Mts

Gobi Desert

Euphrates

Tigris

Karakum
Desert

Taklimakan Desert

EAST
CHINA
SEA

THE GULF

Sichuan
(Szechwan)

Yangtze

Tropic of Cancer

Indus

H I M A L A Y A S

Taiwan

Mt Everest
29 029 ft

Ganges

Irrawaddy

Salween

Mekong

Philippines

BAY OF
BENGAL

SOUTH CHINA SEA

ARABIAN

SEA

Andaman
Islands

Mt Kinabalu
△ 13430 ft

Equator

Sri Lanka

Sumatra

Borneo

Sulawesi
(Celebes)

Java

INDIAN

OCEAN

| 0 | 200 | 400 | 600 | 800 | 1000 miles |

| 0 | 400 | 800 | 1200 | 1600 km |

149

The Himalayas

Above *Crystalline lakes occupy basins in the valley floors, heightening the austere beauty of the surrounding peaks. At such altitudes the temperature is too low to permit plant growth and the land is barren and infertile.*

Left *Mount Everest, glowing here at sunset, is the highest mountain in the world at 29 029 ft (8848 m). Note the cockade of mist and blown snow which has formed to the right of the peak in the wake of the fierce winds that buffet its upper slopes.*

Right *The Karakoram Mountains form the western end of the great Himalayan chain at the point where Pakistan backs onto China. They are among the most rugged mountains in the world, with 60 peaks rising above 22 000 ft (6706 m) in altitude. The snow line is clearly visible on slopes that are too steep and unstable to support more than token vegetation. In the summer silvery rivulets flow along the deep valleys that have been formed by the torrents of water pouring down when the snow melts.*

Left *Fed by melt-water from the snow-covered peaks on the roof of the world, streams of ice-cold water meander across the wide valleys of the Tibetan plateau. Only coarse moorland grasses can withstand the cold at such altitudes and they provide poor grazing for all but the hardiest species of wildlife.*

Above *The ounce, or snow leopard, leads a solitary existence among the rocks and snows of the high mountains from Turkestan and Tibet through to Mongolia. It usually feeds on the wild sheep and goats of these regions, but may take gazelle, deer and pheasants when it descends to the lower valleys to escape the severe winter weather.*

The pear-shaped Indian sub-continent is cut off from the rest of Asia by the impassable barrier of the Himalayan Mountain chain. Yet within its boundaries it offers as varied a range of wildlife as any great continent.

Below *A tigress brings her cubs down to a waterhole to drink. During hot weather tigers may even sit in the water to keep cool. Tigers are the biggest of the cat family, and quite capable of bringing down animals as large as a small elephant. Unrestricted hunting over the centuries has resulted in the virtual extermination of the tiger throughout most of Asia.*

Right *The nilgai is the largest of the Indian antelopes and a favorite prey of the tiger, which inhabits the forests of central India. Only the females form groups: males prefer a more solitary life, except during the breeding season when they fight over the females using their short horns to jab at each other. These duels are often carried out while the combatants are kneeling.*

Left *The Indian one-horned rhino is the largest member of the rhino family, weighing up to 4 tons (4000 kg). It is often accompanied by cattle egrets that pick ticks imbedded in the great folds of skin on the rhino's back or catch insects disturbed by it as it walks through the grass.*

Below left *The Malayan tapir is an inhabitant of the riverbank forests of southeast Asia. An expert swimmer, it can remain submerged underwater for several minutes. Tapirs are strictly vegetarian and are normally solitary.*

Below *Resplendent in their beautiful spotted summer coats, male axis deer dispute their status in the hierarchy by vigorous pushing matches with horns locked. Axis deer occur widely throughout India, where they prefer relatively open forests. Like all large deer, they live in herds that vary greatly in size and composition.*

Southeast Asia

Left *The luxuriant forests of southeast Asia and the islands of the East Indies have the greatest diversity of wildlife of any similar area in the world.*

Far left *The unhasty pace of life of the aptly-named slow loris occurs at night in the lower branches of the forest trees. It is one of several kinds of small primitive primates in the area, and emits twittering bird-like calls as it moves quietly and methodically through the tangled shrubbery searching for insects and fruit.*

Below *Macaques occur throughout southeast Asia, China and India with more than a dozen species represented altogether. The longtailed macaque shown here is one of the most widely distributed species, and occurs throughout the Indo-Chinese peninsula and the islands of the Malay archipelago. Like most monkeys, the female carries her infant clinging to the fur of her belly until it is weaned. Macaques live in troops of 20-50 members and range widely through the forests.*

FLYING ANIMALS OF BORNEO

In the dense forests of southeast Asia, being able to travel directly from one tall tree to the next without having to descend several hundred feet to the ground has considerable advantages. Many species have developed means of remaining airborne so that they can cover the distances between the trees more efficiently. None, however have evolved powered flight; rather, all use extended flaps of skin to create surfaces on which to glide. In many cases these are only crude solutions to the problems of flying and the animals can be said at best to get from tree to tree by means of barely controlled crash-landings.

Although representatives of many of these species occur throughout southeastern Asia, nowhere do they occur with such variety and frequency as they do on the island of Borneo. Of these, the 3 ft (1 m) long flying snake is perhaps the most extraordinary. Able to extend its ribs to make a flattened plane, it gains just enough lift to undertake a controlled dive from the forest trees into the undergrowth below where its somewhat hazardous landing is cushioned by the dense leaf growth.

The flying dragon (really a lizard) has large brightly colored folds of skin around its neck and along the length of its body. When these are extended it is able to glide between the trees in search of insects.

The distance record, however, goes to the flying lemur. This cat-sized mammal has an elastic membrane running from its chin to the tip of its tail. By stretching out its arms and legs, it can make a perfect gliding platform on which to sail distances of up to 450 ft (137 m) through the forest.

Flying squirrels also glide on flaps of skin stretched between their limbs. Less accomplished fliers than the flying lemurs, they can nonetheless glide distances of up to 200 ft (61 m). Some species can be as long as 3 ft (1 m). Flying foxes, on the other hand, are neither foxes nor gliders: they are in fact giant fruit bats and do rely on powered flight.

Top right *This flying snake is also known as the paradise tree snake.*

Right *The flying dragon is actually a lizard.*

Below *The flying lemur glides from tree to tree using an extended elastic membrane.*

Far right *The flying frog has enlarged webs between its elongated toes which it can extend to form a primitive parachute.*

Below *The Komodo dragon is really a giant lizard. This heavily built reptile can grow up to 10 ft (3 m) in length, making it a formidable opponent. Like all lizards, it is carnivorous and will eat almost any kind of meat. Komodo dragons are generally active during the day and spend the night in dens in rocky outcrops. They are found only on the East Indian islands of Komodo, Rinja and Flores to the east of Java.*

Right *The delicately patterned clouded leopard is probably the most beautiful as well as the smallest of the leopards. It is widespread throughout India, China and southeast Asia, where it inhabits dense jungle, spending most of its time in the crowns of large trees. It preys mainly on birds and small mammals.*

Far right *Southeast Asia and its outlying islands are characterized by parallel series of steep-sided mountains that are separated by deep valleys. The dense jungles are often almost impenetrable and travel is possible only up the fast-flowing rivers.*

Above *The atlas moth is one of the largest flying insects alive today, with a wingspan of nearly 10 in (25 cm). The male's feathered antennae are designed to be able to detect the female's scents even at the very faintest concentrations in the air.*

Left *Many of the islands in the Malay archipelago have active volcanoes. In Indonesia, Mt Bromo raises its ridged cone above the lava-strewn plain to a height of 2581 ft (787 m).*

Top left *Hornbills are remarkable for the often massive casques above their bills. During the breeding season the female is walled up in a hollow tree until the eggs have hatched and the young are ready to fly, while her mate feeds her by passing food through a small opening in the mud-walled entrance to the nest. The species shown here is the giant hornbill, common throughout southeast Asia.*

Left *The ferocious Philippines monkey-eating eagle, an extremely skilled flier for so large a bird, can fly speedily between the tangled branches of the forest to snatch unsuspecting monkeys from the tree tops.*

Right *Pythons are among the most primitive of the snakes and possess a pair of tiny claw-like projections either side of the pelvis: these are the remnants of the hindlegs that the snakes' ancestors once possessed. This green tree python from New Guinea guards its clutch of eggs, the first of which are just starting to hatch*

Below *The rafflesia is the largest flower in the world, and lives as a parasite on the roots of vines. Only its fleshy 18 in (45 cm) flower-head is visible above the ground. This 15 lb (7 kg) monster is hardly suitable for suburban gardens: it smells of rotting flesh and is pollinated by the myriad flies attracted by the stench.*

MANGROVE SWAMPS

Along the tidal creeks and inundated coastal mudflats of southeast Asia and its fringing islands, mangrove trees weave their tangled roots into dense impenetrable forests. These remarkable trees, rarely more than 10 ft (3 m) tall, have an extremely hard wood that is resistant to salt water. As a result, they can tolerate living below the high tide line where their roots and lower stems are frequently immersed in the sea.

Mangrove produce both the usual kind of underground roots and roots that grow out from the trunk of the tree itself. The latter arch out at an angle, entering the ground some distance from the tree and forming a tangled mass on which the tree seems to sit. Under the mud, the roots travel outwards sending up tough spikes into the air. These aerial roots have minute openings in them through which the tree can "breathe" oxygen.

New tree trunks may grow directly from the underground roots so the mangroves spread rapidly in dense thickets, but they can also reproduce by seeds in the usual way. These begin to germinate on the tree, developing long spikes that hang downwards. When the seed is finally released, the spike is driven into the mud by its own weight, so that the seed is firmly rooted and can begin to grow.

The mangrove swamps are home for one of the most unusual species of fish, the mudskipper. A member of the widespread goby family, these fishes can breathe air by trapping it in their enlarged gill chambers, enabling them to skip about on the exposed mud at low tide, propelled by their limb-like pectoral fins.

Left *Mangrove trees on the coast of Malaysia.*

Far left *A male mudskipper displays with fins erect and "arms" extended near the breeding pool in order to attract a mate.*

Below *Mudskippers frequently like to rest out of the water on mangrove stumps.*

Deserts

Left *The barren uplands of Cappadocia in Turkey are part of a long chain of deserts and dry plains that stretch all the way from Arabia and Asia Minor eastwards, across the northern foothills of the Himalayas into China and Mongolia. Quite different to the popular conception of sandy areas full of dunes, the dry plains of Cappadocia with their sparse covering of grass are typical of the deserts of central Asia.*

Below *The kulan or Asiatic wild ass roams the vast expanses of the Asian high plateau from Mongolia through into Iran. The speed and toughness of this relatively rare animal allow it to eke out a precarious existence on the sparse grassland vegetation.*

Bottom *The two-humped Bactrian camel still survives in the wild in Mongolia's Gobi desert. The camel can live on almost any kind of food if necessary and is able to withstand great extremes of temperature. Its humps are used to store fat, not water, as is commonly supposed.*

Siberia and Mongolia

Right *The swamp forests of the taiga extend in a broad sweep along the northern foot of the Siberian plateau, to separate the highland from tundra plains on the Arctic coast. Low mountains with dense forests alternate with water-logged boulder-strewn valleys that support only scrubby vegetation.*

Below *The rolling hills of Mongolia support only a sparse vegetation cover.*

Below right *Przewalski's horse, a small stocky relative of the domesticated species, is the only truly wild horse. It was discovered roaming the plains of western Mongolia as recently as 1879, but subsequently became extinct in the wild. Successful breeding of the species in captivity could result in its being reintroduced into its native homeland.*

173

Japan

Above *This sunset view of Japan from Mount Norikura-dake looks like a typically Japanese painting.*

Far right *Wild cherry blossom adds a touch of spring to the steep Japanese hillsides. Japan is one of the most mountainous countries in the world, with more than 80 per cent of its land surface too steep to cultivate.*

Right *The Japanese macaque is the most northerly species of primate in the world. On Honshu Island in the north of the Japanese archipelago the monkeys face harsh winters with heavy snowfalls. One particular population on the Shiga plateau has learned how to keep warm during the winter by sitting in the numerous volcanic hot-springs that occur in the area.*

China

Right *The heavily forested mountains of Szechwan in western China support large tracts of bamboo, the only food eaten by the giant pandas (far right) that live here. These rather bear-like relatives of the raccoons are now among the most endangered species in the world. Pandas spend up to 12 hours a day feeding, mainly on the leaves and shoots of bamboo. They are almost completely ground-living, leading quiet lives in the mist-shrouded mountains where their only enemy is man.*

Bottom right *The giant panda's smaller relative, the lesser or red panda, clearly shows its close relationship with the raccoon family. It, too, is vegetarian, though it does occasionally eat birds and their eggs. The red panda is only a little larger than a cat, living in trees in the forests of Tibet and western China, where it is active only at night.*

Australasia

Australasia is the smallest of the seven continents, but it was originally much larger. What were once its northern and eastern sides have sunk below the sea, leaving only a chain of islands. These extend in a great arc from New Guinea in the north, through the scattered islands of the Solomon, New Hebrides and New Caledonia groups, to New Zealand in the southeast.

Almost everything about the Australasian block is unusual. The rocks of the Australian mainland are among the oldest on earth, its few mountain ranges being the greatly eroded stumps of the earth's earliest period of mountain building. Because it was spared the later periods of mountain building that produced the great fold mountains of the New and Old Worlds – the Rockies, Andes, Alps and Himalayas – it has no high mountains. Much of the continent is flat and its highest peak is Mt Kosciusko, a mere 7316 ft (2230 m), just a quarter the height of Everest.

Lake Disappointment

Aside from the narrow strip along the southeastern coasts where rainfall is high, the continent is made up almost entirely of immense dry steppes and sandy deserts. In the middle of Australia the low MacDonnell Ranges provide a focal center from which dry river beds fan out into the surrounding deserts. These encircle it like the spokes of a great wheel, the Great Sandy, the Gibson (with its poignantly named Lake Disappointment), the Great Victoria, the Nullarbor (literally "null-arbor": "no tree"), the Simpson and the Tanami deserts. Much of the rest of the landscape is arid acacia thornscrub or eucalyptus bush. Only on the well watered plains of the southeast and the north, and in the eastern mountains, do forests occur.

Dry rivers

Australia is by far the most arid of the inhabited continental landmasses with two-thirds of the continent receiving less than 20 in (50 cm) of rainfall a year. Even its two greatest rivers, the Murray and the Darling, have been known to dry up occasionally. The population is concentrated in the wetter coastal areas, leaving great tracts of land as empty wilderness.

Much of the Australian vegetation is unique. The eucalypts (member of the myrtle family) that so typify the country occur in more than 600 species, ranging from small flowering plants, through the stunted "mallee" scrub of the desert areas, to the great blue gums, whose tall

The Olgas rise unexpectedly from the surrounding scrubland of the Uluru National Park in Australia's Northern Territory.

straight trunks rise 200 ft (60 m) or more above the ground. Like almost everything in Australia, the eucalypts are highly adapted to dry conditions. Capable of growing at rates of several feet a year, they are adept at finding and absorbing any water that may be present in the soil, while their thick leathery leaves prevent too much loss through evaporation.

Pouched mammals
It is clear that most of Australia's animals must have entered the continent at some very early stage during the evolution of the higher animals, for its native mammal fauna consists almost entirely of the marsupials or pouched mammals, and the primitive egg-laying monotremes, the only surviving members of this family of earliest mammals.

Apart from bats, there are no native placental mammals of the kind that evolved later and came to dominate the rest of the world. Placental mammals represent an advance on the marsupials in evolutionary terms, the main difference being that the baby spends its entire period of development inside the mother's womb. By contrast, young marsupials emerge at a very early stage, when they are no more than embryos, and crawl through their mother's fur to the pouch on the mother's belly, where they are nourished by milk while completing their development.

The kangaroo and koala are the two best-known species of Australian wildlife. Yet there are many other extraordinary native marsupials, such as wallabies, wombats, small marsupial rats, tree kangaroos, bandicoots and possums, as well as the tiger cats and carnivorous mongoose-like quolls.

Tasmanian devil
Two marsupial carnivores, the Tasmanian devil and the thylacine, were once found throughout the continent, but owing to human persecution and competition from dingos – the wild descendants of domesticated dogs introduced by Australian Aborigines – they are now confined to the island of Tasmania, off the continent's southeastern tip. The Tasmanian devil is the marsupial equivalent of the hyena though much smaller. It is a scavenger as well as a hunter. The thylacine, or Tasmanian wolf, is not a wolf at all, but resembles a wolf or dog in both appearance and behavior because of its similar way of life. Although it was thought to have become extinct in the 1930s, signs of it are still occasionally seen in the more remote and inaccessible parts of the thickly forested Tasmanian mountains. It is thought to be the rarest animal in the world.

Living fossils
Even more primitive than the marsupials are Australia's unique egg-laying mammals, the monotremes, of which only the echidna and the duck-billed platypus survive. These curious animals are the last remnants of the ancient link between the mammals and the egg-laying reptiles.

When platypus skins were first brought back to Europe, they were thought to be hoaxes, made up from different animals: the body, head and feet of an otter-like creature combined with the beak from some gigantic species of waterfowl. Although the platypus can move well on land, it is much more at home in water where its wide bill is used to poke around in the mud of river and lake beds in search of crayfish, worms and small fish.

Frilled lizards and lyrebirds
Australia also boasts a number of remarkable species of fish, reptiles and birds. The primitive lungfish with its lung pouches instead of gills is a relic of the earliest groups of fishes. Frilled lizards expand great collars around their necks to frighten off would-be attackers. The mallee fowl builds a huge mound of twigs and vegetation into which the female places her eggs: the interior generates its own heat by fermentation, and the male maintains the temperature at a constant level by opening and closing air vents, using his tongue as a thermometer.

In the giant eucalyptus forests of the south, the lyrebird spreads its long delicate tail feathers into the shape of a lyre while courting a female and bowerbirds attract a mate by decorating their elaborate twig bowers with shells, feathers and other colored objects.

Many of Australia's animals, or their close relatives, occur in the dense tropical forests of the continent's northern outpost, the island of New Guinea. This huge island differs quite markedly from the Australian mainland: it is dominated by snow-capped mountain chains that rise to heights of 16 000 ft (4900 m).

Forests in the clouds
Probably one of the wettest places on earth, New Guinea's mountains are shrouded in a permanent mist of drizzle or cloud during the rainy season. The dense tropical rainforests that clothe this rugged island are so impenetrable that their Stone Age inhabitants remained undiscovered until the 1930s, and even now there may still be tribes in central New Guinea that are unknown to the outside world.

New Guinea's links with the Australian mainland were severed as recently as a million years ago, whereas its last links with the islands of the Malaysian archipelago to the west were much more remote. Its animals are consequently Australian rather than Asian. It has several species of echidnas and 84 marsupial species, including ground- and tree-living kangaroos, bandicoots and the sugar glider (a flying possum).

Nonetheless, because New Guinea is close to the Asian islands, more advanced land mammals have occasionally managed to cross the narrow sea channel that separates it from the Celebes and Moluccas. These have included several species of squirrels, rats and mice, though nothing larger than a small pig has been able to pass across.

Birds of paradise
The most spectacular and exotic wild animals in New Guinea are not mammals but birds: the birds of paradise, which also occur on the adjacent islands, but nowhere in quite the same variety and splendor as here. The males of these species have the most dazzling plumage of any living bird, with brilliant colors, gossamer-like tail feathers, long head-plumes or tail-streamers and magnificent epaulettes and crests.

At the southern end of the Australasian island chain lies the New Zealand group, two large islands with many smaller ones around them. Their position on the edge of the sunken continent has left them vulnerable to a variety of geological processes, and active volcanoes, hot springs, geysers and mud volcanoes abound, especially in North Island. South Island consists almost entirely of a chain of mountains, the Southern Alps, that rises to heights of 11 000 ft (3350 m).

Islands on the edge of the world
New Zealand's position on the edge of the world has resulted in relatively few species of animals reaching it. It has no native mammals, other than two species of bat, but there are now substantial populations of Himalayan tahr, European red deer, wild boar, feral goats and rabbits as a result of introductions made by the early settlers. These foreign species have played havoc with the island's native fauna, particularly the birds, of which there are only 23 species, most of them unique to New Zealand.

New Zealand is particularly famous for its flightless birds, like the kiwi with its long curving bill, and the now extinct giant moa, an ostrich-like bird that stood 12 ft (4 m) high. It also has a number of unusual parrots, such as the nocturnal kakapo and the green kea. The hawk-like kea will attack sheep, but despite persecution by farmers it is still abundant, thanks to the remoteness of its preferred habitat in the Southern Alps.

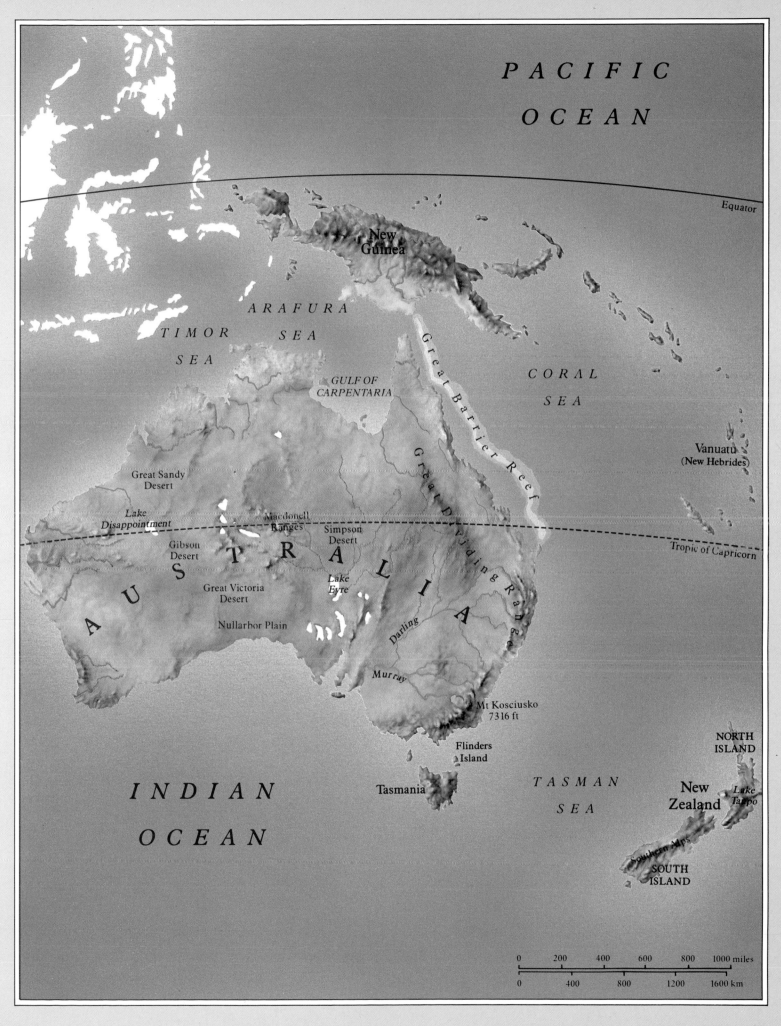

PACIFIC

OCEAN

Equator

New
Guinea

ARAFURA

SEA

TIMOR

SEA

GULF OF
CARPENTARIA

CORAL

SEA

Vanuatu
(New Hebrides)

Great Sandy
Desert

Lake
Disappointment

Macdonell
Ranges

Simpson
Desert

Tropic of Capricorn

Gibson
Desert

AUSTRALIA

Great Victoria
Desert

Lake
Eyre

Nullarbor Plain

Darling

Murray

Mt Kosciusko
7316 ft

Flinders
Island

INDIAN

Tasmania

TASMAN

SEA

NORTH
ISLAND

New
Zealand

Lake
Taupo

OCEAN

Southern Alps

SOUTH
ISLAND

| 0 | 200 | 400 | 600 | 800 | 1000 miles |

| 0 | 400 | 800 | 1200 | 1600 km |

Polynesian Islands

Right *The Pacific contains an extraordinary number of palm-fringed islands, far more than any other ocean. Some of these islands are of coral origin, having been built up over many thousands of years by tiny coral polyps. These polyps build their homes in great colonies close to the surface in well-lit waters.*

Far right *The wobbygong is a bottom-living shark commonly found in the waters between Australia and Japan.*

Below *Raiatea in the Polynesian chain is of volcanic origin. This type of island tends to be mountainous and the rich volcanic soils support luxuriant vegetation. Even these, however, often have fringing coral reefs around them, providing sheltered harbors.*

BIRDS OF PARADISE

The birds of paradise are generally acknowledged to be the most beautiful birds in the world, although ironically they are related to the crow family. Of the total 43 species known to science, 35 occur only in New Guinea. These spectacular birds range from the size of a thrush to that of a magpie, and have developed nuptial ornamentation to its finest heights. During the breeding season the males gather in special trees where they display to the females, showing off their exotically plumed fans and ruffs in irridescent displays that are fantastic and sometimes almost bizarre.

Hanging upside down, the blue bird of paradise seems more like a hand-crafted ornament than a living bird, yet sitting quietly on a branch it looks unexceptional. Many species have a pair of greatly elongated wire-like tail feathers, others like the "standard wings" have pale ribbon-like streamers rising from the wing joints and the flagbirds have stiff wires tipped with feathers rising from behind the eyes.

Right *New Guinea's steep-sided mountains are clothed in impenetrable jungle. This is the home of the birds of paradise.*

Below *The blue bird of paradise, sometimes known as Crown Prince Rudolph's bird.*

Far right *This magnificent bird of paradise with its elongated tail feathers comes from Papua New Guinea.*

Below right *The raggiana bird of paradise hangs upside down from a branch in a mating display.*

New Zealand

Below *The profusion of hot springs and outflows from the geysers provide fertile breeding grounds for algae that encrust the rocks around the outlets.*

During the last century, the geysers declined steadily until they ceased functioning altogether by 1880. Then, in 1886 Mt Tarawera erupted, destroying many renowned geological features in the area and opening up an enormous chasm in the ground 9 miles (14.5 km) long.

Seven gigantic geysers came into existence during the course of all this, some of which threw columns of steam, mud and stones 800 ft (250 m) into the air.

Right *New Zealand's North Island is an area of intense volcanic activity lying on the junction of the submerged Australian continental shelf and the Pacific Ocean floor. Some of the most spectacular geysers and mud volcanoes in the world are found on this island which beat time with regular pulses of steam-heated water and mud. Many are concentrated in a 5000 sq. mile (12 950 sq. km) area around Lake Taupo, a huge lake occupying a pumice-covered plain in the island's center.*

Far right *In the Waiotapu area the Lady Know geyser jets scalding water and steam high into the air.*

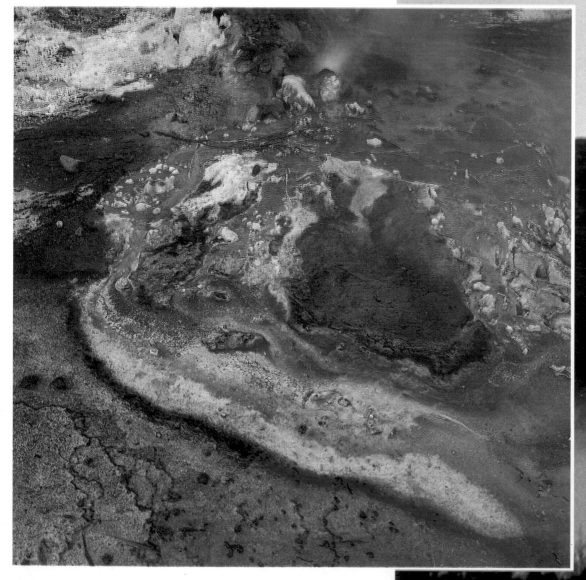

Australia

Below *The cassowary is a large flightless bird related to the ostriches. It occurs in forests throughout New Guinea and the neighboring islands, down as far as the northern corner of Australia. Its rudimentary wings are no use at all, but its legs are very stout and can be used to good effect in self-defence. The common cassowary, which has a horny helmet on its head, lives in pairs on the forest floor, where it feeds on fruits and herbs and the occasional small animal.*

Right *The emu is a native of the drier open grasslands of the Australian outback and is second tallest bird after the ostrich. More sociable than the closely related cassowary, it lives in small groups. During the breeding season the male emits a loud booming note as part of his mating display.*

Far right *The male emu is responsible for incubating the eggs. Up to 12 eggs are laid by the female in a shallow hole.*

THE GREAT BARRIER REEF

The Great Barrier Reef is the longest continuous mass of coral in the world. It stretches for 1250 miles (2000 km) from the southern tip of New Guinea down the eastern seaboard of Australia as far as Sandy Cape: the water is too cold for coral to grow beyond that. The reef itself lies in water that is only about 300 ft (90 m) deep, having been built up slowly by the growth of coral organisms as the sea bed gradually sunk beneath the waves.

Coral is formed from the hard external skeleton of millions of tiny creatures, the coral polyps. As these die off, they leave behind a rock-like skeleton which forms a bedrock on which the next generation of polyps build their chambers. Corals cannot grow in water depths greater than about 150 ft (45 m), so, as the sea bed sinks, the corals build up the level of the reef.

Coral reefs grow outwards from the coast. The outer Pacific face of the Barrier Reef is therefore the most active, growing steadily eastwards in a nearly perpendicular wall. Behind it, the surface and inner faces of the reef grow in a slower, more haphazard fashion. Here there are exotically branched non-reef-forming corals.

The Barrier Reef is a bewildering riot of color and movement. There is nothing else like it on earth. And in addition to the spectacular corals there is an astounding variety of brilliantly colored creatures. Oysters and molluscs grow to all shapes and sizes; sea urchins lurch about on their myriad arms, while starfish litter the reef surface along with other extraordinary creatures like sea cucumbers, sponges and anemones.

Sharks streak through the water like gray torpedoes in their search for prey. The great white ghost of the 60 ft (18 m) whale shark glides effortlessly by, while manta rays, their wing-like fins growing to widths of 20 ft (6 m), seek plankton and small fish.

The reef is extremely dangerous for the unwary. Not only are there sharks, but also poisonous jellyfish and sea snails, marauding barracuda and moray eels. Sea serpents grow to lengths of 6 ft (2 m) and lurk among the coral beds waiting for prey to swim within reach of their venomous fangs.

Divers not frightened off by such dangers find the waters packed with a stunning array of fish life: massive groupers and sunfishes, flamboyant parrotfish and clownfish, delicately shaded angel fish, all attracted to the reef by abundant food supplies.

Above right *A blue shark slips through the sunlit water in search of prey. Sharks are sophisticated hunters: when they close in for the kill their eyes are protected by a membrane. They attack blind, guided unerringly by an acute sensory system.*

Above far right *Despite its ungainly appearance, the hawksbill turtle is an excellent swimmer.*

Right *Shoals of fish like these slate bream throng the reef, preyed on by sharks.*

Far right *A hammerhead shark, one of the most ferocious hunters in the deep.*

Above *Giant clams grow to more than 3 ft (1 m) in diameter and can weigh up to 450 lbs (200 kg). Once they have settled on a spot and begun to grow, they soon become too big to move again.*

Left *Silhouetted against the opening of a cave in the coral, reef fish circle lazily in the clear turquoise water.*

Right *The coral of the Great Barrier Reef is being slowly killed by the crown-of-thorns starfish. But the starfish itself occasionally falls prey to predators like this triton that can get past spiny defences.*

Far right *The nautilus has remained almost unchanged since life began in the sea.*

Above *Most large fish depend on cleaner fishes that specialize in removing parasites and fungi from their skin. Here a cleaner wrasse fearlessly enters the mouth cavity of its client, a coral trout, to clean around its teeth.*

Left *The deadly lionfish with its poisonous spines hides among the coral stems and lies in wait for passing prey.*

Above right *Life on the reef is full of danger: a cup coral has caught a small fish. Once engulfed in its sack-like stomach the fish will be digested by the coral.*

Right *Two gaudy nudibranchs mate amid the corals.*

Trees

Australian vegetation is dominated by the eucalyptus or gum tree, a unique family of trees related to the myrtles and all but confined to the Australian continent and the nearby island of Tasmania. The long pointed leaves that typify the eucalyptus are highly aromatic and produce an oil that has become widely used as an inhalant. Eucalypts are among the fastest growing of all trees and are well adapted to the dry conditions of the Australian continent where rainfall is often very irregular. One species, the blue gum, has been introduced into every other continent as a fast-growing source of timber for building and for fuel.

Right *The gnarled trunks of the river gum straggle across the meadows of the Flinders Range in southern Australia.*

Below right *The crimson rosella is one of the most striking members of a family that is widespread throughout the Australian woodlands.*

Below *The cockatoos are one of the most characteristic groups of Australian parrots, distinguished by the crest which can be raised at will. They live in flocks in the woods where they feed on fruits and insects. This gang-gang cockatoo from the southeast is extracting seeds from a pod.*

Left *The mountain ash, the largest of the eucalyptus trees, grows in lush forests in the mountains of southeastern Australia. The trunks grow to heights of up to 200 ft (60 m). One of the characteristic features of the eucalyptus is its papery bark that peels off in strips.*

Right *Tucking its abdomen between its legs, a bulldog ant pauses to groom itself. At the tip of its abdomen is a sting capable of delivering a painful wound.*

Below *Green tree ants build their nests by stitching together a bundle of leaves hanging from a branch to make an enclosed capsule. While one group of ants holds the edges of two leaves together, other ants "glue" the leaves in place using silk produced by their larvae.*

Left *Cockatoos are a distinctive group of parrots confined to Australia and the nearby islands. Altogether there are some 17 species, including the pink cockatoo from southeastern Australia shown here.*

Above *During the breeding season, the male lyrebird scratches up a little hillock of soil on which he stands to display to passing females. Lyrebirds live in the very densest bush, and because of this they have a highly developed song to attract the females to them. One of the best mimics in the bird world, they can faithfully reproduce almost any sound from the roar of a chain-saw to the intricate calls of other birds and animals.*

Right *The laughing jackass or kookaburra, surely the most famous of the Australian birds, is a member of the kingfisher family. Like all kingfishers, it nests in sandbanks, bringing food back to its young once they hatch. This one has caught a lizard.*

Above *The thrush-sized bowerbird is related to the birds of paradise. Here a male decorates his display area with a collection of flowers, fruits, shells, feathers and colored pebbles in order to attract females during the breeding season. Some species also construct elaborate bowers with twigs. After mating, the female lays her two eggs in a bulky nest built high in a tree some distance away.*

Right *In the low mountains of the southeast, the rivers cut through luxuriant forests. These streams are the home of the strangest of all animals, the unique duck-billed platypus.*

Far right *Seemingly part duck and part otter, the platypus is one of the most primitive of all the mammals. It lays leathery eggs rather similar to those of many reptiles. When the young hatch out, they are fed on milk secreted directly through pores in the mother's skin rather than through specialized mammary glands as in other mammals. The platypus is a very fast swimmer, although awkward on land.*

202

MARSUPIALS

The marsupial mammals of Australia are the descendants of the original primitive mammals that inhabited the earth some 60 million or so years ago. When Australia became separated from the other great continents shortly after that time, its primitive mammals survived while those elsewhere became extinct because they were unable to compete with the newly evolved placental mammals.

Marsupials differ from the more advanced placental mammals in a number of ways, the most important being that the young are born very premature and complete their development in a special fur-lined pouch on the mother's belly. At birth, the young of even the largest species of kangaroos are no more than 1 inch (2.5 cm) long. Hairless, blind and with only head and shoulders well developed, the infant is little more than a partially developed fetus.

Even at this stage it is able to crawl unaided from its mother's birth canal up across her stomach and into her pouch, where it fastens itself onto a large teat and remains fixed there until it has completed its development. Once it reaches the stage at which a placental mammal would be born, it uses the pouch as a place of refuge from which to explore the outside world.

Many marsupials possess the remarkable ability to halt the development of a newly conceived fetus and to retain it in a state of suspended animation in the womb. This only occurs when there is insufficient food available for the mother to be able to rear her baby, and is an adaptation to the harsh conditions often found in Australia.

Below The jerboa marsupial mouse that feeds on insects.

Right A brush-tailed rock wallaby with its young.

Below right The Tasmanian devil is now practically extinct, due to man's encroachment on its forest home.

Far right Koala bears are strictly vegetarian, eating the leaves of only one species of eucalyptus.

Scrubland and Desert

Right *One of Australia's many species of cockatoo, the crow-sized little corella inhabits the eucalyptus woodlands of northern Australia, where it sometimes forms flocks several thousand birds strong.*

Below *The tree goanna is one of many large monitor lizards found throughout the Old World. The goanna is an inhabitant of the drier scrub areas of Australia, and an excellent tree-climber.*

Below right *An inhabitant of the deserts and thornscrub, the frilled lizard suddenly extends a flap of skin around its neck when alarmed. This serves to frighten off predators, both by startling them and by making the lizard seem larger and more formidable than it really is.*

Main picture *In the dry eucalyptus-dotted grasslands of northeastern Australia, termites build their pillar-like nests out of sand grains cemented together by saliva. This mixture sets like concrete and is virtually impregnable.*

Below right *Australia's other primitive egg-laying mammal, the spiny echidna, lives in the arid grasslands where it uses its powerful clawed forelegs to tear open termite nests. Like all anteaters it lacks teeth and has a long sticky tongue on which it catches ants and other insects.*

Right *A red kangaroo male can stand 8 ft (2.5 m) tall, making it one of the largest of the marsupials. Kangaroos live in the dry grasslands of the continent's eastern interior, and cover huge distances in search of food. They are normally rather solitary, but gather in large groups where grass has sprouted after a local rain shower.*

Preceding page *The Pinnacles in western Australia are the result of rocky outcrops being "drowned" in the desert's creeping sands.*

Above *This thick-tailed gecko is walking on outstretched legs to keep itself off the burning sands of the desert.*

Right *A blotched bluetongue skink gives birth to live young. Some species of bluetongue skinks grow to lengths of 2 ft (60 cm).*

Far right *Ayers Rock, Australia's most famous natural feature, is renowned for its ability to reflect the subtle shades of the sky's changing colors.*

212

Antarctica

The fourth largest of the continents, Antarctica was not discovered until 1772 when it was sighted by Captain Cook. Even so, no one succeeded in landing on the mainland itself until Captain Ross reached it in 1840. The last great unexplored landmass on the globe, Antarctica is the most isolated continent: while it is possible to reach every other continent without having to cross more than 60 miles (95 km) of shallow sea, Antarctica can be reached only after crossing more than 600 miles (950 km) of water of oceanic depth through some of the stormiest seas in the world.

Whereas more than one million people, a large number of animals and vast tracts of coniferous forest are to be found within the Arctic Circle in the northern hemisphere, the comparable area below the Antarctic Circle is all but devoid of life. The only land animals to breed on this great southern wasteland are a few species of insects, but the seas are alive with sea mammals, penguins and other fish-eating birds.

Ice-bound continent

This striking contrast between the fertility of the two polar regions is due to the isolation of Antarctica. In the northern hemisphere huge continental masses break up the oceans, pushing warm sea currents up towards the Arctic Circle which heat up the bordering continental coasts in the process. As a result, the southern tip of Spitsbergen remains ice-free despite being nearly 15° of latitude above the Arctic Circle.

At the other end of the earth, the Antarctic continent is perpetually under ice, seven million cubic miles (29 million cubic km) of it all told: something like 90 per cent of the ice on this planet. The surface rises to a flat plateau at an altitude of around 10 000 ft (3050m) in the region of the South Pole itself. The ice cap is about 6500 ft (1980 m) thick on average, but here and there the peaks of great mountain chains raise areas of bare rock above the surrounding snow fields. Of the continent's total land surface of some five million square miles (13 million square km), less than 100 square miles (260 square km) is permanently free of ice.

A frozen desert

The climate is too cold for precipitation to fall as anything except snow, but overall the continent receives little more than 1 ft (30 cm) of snow a year. This is equivalent to about 7 in (18 cm) of rain, an amount that would produce desert conditions in the tropics.

The most northerly point of the Antarctic peninsula perfectly mirrored in the still icy waters of the Southern Ocean.

At one time, it was suggested that the ice cap was in fact shrinking, but the latest information indicates that it is probably in a state of equilibrium. Were the ice cap to melt entirely, however, sea levels would rise all over the world and a great many major cities and centers of population would be drowned. The shape of the Antarctic continent would also change radically if the ice cap melted, for in reality much of what appears as land is ice-covered sea. Without its ice cap, Antarctica would be reduced to a mainland area of about half its present size, with a string of islands on the Pacific side.

Coldest place on earth

Antarctica is by far the coldest of the continents. Even at its most northerly point, the average temperature over the whole year seldom rises much above 5°F (−15°C), well below freezing. During the summer temperatures rarely exceed freezing point in many places on the continent and the lowest temperature ever recorded was −127°F (−88°C) at Vostok in the Russian sector of Antarctica. For consistently low temperatures, however, the coldest place on earth is the "Pole of Cold" with an average annual temperature of −72°F (−58°C), 16°F (9°C) colder than the true South Pole.

Throughout the winter months, Antarctica is ravaged by blizzards. With no large blocks of land to impede the path of the wind, it circles round the southern hemisphere with unabated ferocity in the latitudes of 40°–60°, known as the "Roaring Forties" and the "Furious Fifties". These winds combine with the peculiar weather conditions created by intense cold to generate blizzards of unrivaled severity, especially on the coastal margins. Parts of the continent experience winds that average 50 mph (80 km/h) as a normal part of daily life, and winds in excess of 150 mph (240 km/h) have been recorded in particularly severe storms. During blizzards, the wind whips up the loose surface snow to create a "white out" and visibility is then reduced to no more than arm's length, even though the sky above is perfectly clear with brilliant sunshine.

Prehistoric life

The Antarctic is devoid of plant life, except for a few lichens and mosses. Yet large coal deposits and fossilized trees have been discovered on the continent, indicating that at some time in the distant past, the Antarctic mainland experienced a very much warmer and wetter climate than it does now. Millions of years ago Antarctica was populated by various species of reptiles and amphibians, now extinct, whose petrified remains can still be seen in the ancient rocks.

Seas of ice

Throughout the year, the larger Antarctic bays are filled by floating ice sheets, the best known of which is the Great Ice Barrier, or Ross Ice Shelf. This massive wall of ice, anything from 50–200 ft (15–60 m) high, blocks the inner part of the bay formed by the Ross Sea, covering an area as large as France. The ice sheet is between 500 and 1500 ft (150 and 450 m) thick and moves outwards towards the sea at a rate of about 500 ft (150 m) a year, fed by numerous glaciers that begin on the South Polar plateau, descending through the Queen Maud and Queen Alexandra mountains, and into the ice shelf.

While the ice sheet's outer end floats freely on the open sea, its landward end is firmly anchored to the glaciers that feed it and there it rests on solid ground. The glaciers of the Antarctic are of magnificent proportions. The Beardmore, one of the largest, is 100 miles (160 km) long. At its head, it is 40 miles (64 km) wide, though the great mass of ice is crushed into a narrow neck only 8 miles (13 km) wide at its base.

Monster icebergs

The surface of the ice sheet is smooth, and the icebergs formed by the break-up of its seaward end have a characteristic "table top" appearance. The ice front presented to the sea is a massive 400 miles (640 km) long, so icebergs formed from the ice sheet are often of immense size. Monsters more than 30 miles (48 km) long are by no means unknown in the waters around the Antarctic. These floating islands drift out into the southern oceans at the mercy of the winds and currents, until they disintegrate in the warmer and stormier waters anything up to 1000 miles (1600 km) to the north.

Such ice sheets are quite different from the sea ice that builds up on the surface of the sea all around the continent during the winter. The surface of the sea begins freezing over as early as February in the more sheltered bays, and continues to increase in thickness until October or November, by which time it may be 7 ft (2 m) thick. Then the slightly warmer temperatures of the Antarctic summer, combined with the action of wind and wave, are sufficient to break up the ice. It disperses into the ocean currents as dense jostling pack-ice that forms a ring around the southern continent.

Rich harvests in the cold ocean

The warm ocean currents penetrating into cold Antarctic waters create ideal conditions for the microscopic plankton. With the plentiful nutrients found in these waters and the perpetual sunlight of the southern summer, their growth is unin-

terrupted and they multiply enormously. This rich growth is feasted on by many small creatures, such as the shrimp-like krill which abound in the chilly waters. These, in turn, are preyed on by fish, whales, and some seabirds.

So abundant do fish become in the summer that millions of birds and seals are attracted by the rich pickings to be had. Penguins, petrels and albatrosses come down to breed on the rocky sub-antarctic islands and mainland shores, while the Arctic tern flies across the globe from the Arctic, thus experiencing constant daylight for most of the year.

Seal summer

Seals are also drawn to the Antarctic during the summer in order to breed, and they may haul out onto the ice flows and beaches to sleep in the summer sun. There are no land predators on the Antarctic, so the seals of that region are much less nervous than those of the Arctic, where polar bears, which are excellent swimmers, are a constant threat as they prowl for a meal of seals or fish.

The only mammalian predator to threaten the seals is the sea leopard, a large species of seal that can grow up to 12 ft (3.7 m) long. It preys primarily on penguins when they are feeding out at sea. Penguin nesting colonies also attract a host of bird predators, including skuas and sheathbills. These become a perennial nuisance at the penguins' nests, destroying eggs and killing the defenceless chicks when the parents are away.

Perpetual night

During the perpetual night of the long Antarctic winter the plankton cease to multiply, and the marine food is no longer replenished. By mid-winter, food is very scarce and most species prefer to migrate into warmer waters further north rather than spend the winter ice-bound. Only the emperor penguin and a few seals remain in Antarctic waters throughout the winter.

Weddell seals are unique in their ability to swim long distances under the sea ice, using their teeth to keep blow-holes open at points where they want to surface. How they find these holes again remains a mystery.

Even more bizarre, however, is the behavior of the emperor penguin, which chooses to breed during the darkness of the Antarctic winter. Its egg is laid in May and incubated for two months by the fasting male bird who huddles with other males for warmth and shelter as the winter blizzards rage around them. Once the chick hatches, the male feeds it on a special milk-like secretion until the female returns with its first meal of fish.

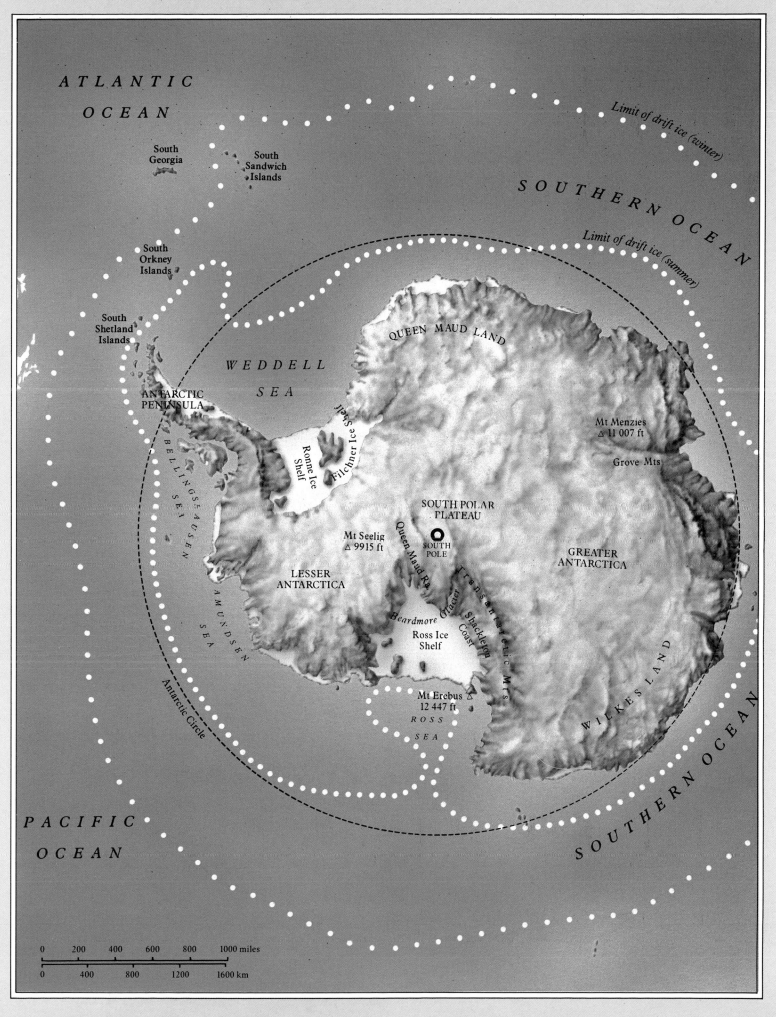

ATLANTIC
OCEAN

SOUTHERN OCEAN

Limit of drift ice (winter)

South
Georgia

South
Sandwich
Islands

Limit of drift ice (summer)

South
Orkney
Islands

QUEEN MAUD LAND

WEDDELL

South
Shetland
Islands

SEA

ANTARCTIC
PENINSULA

Mt Menzies
△ 11 007 ft

Grove Mts

BELLINGSHAUSEN SEA

Ronne Ice
Shelf

Filchner Ice Shelf

SOUTH POLAR
PLATEAU

GREATER
ANTARCTICA

Mt Seelig
△ 9915 ft

Queen Maud Ra.

⊙
SOUTH
POLE

LESSER
ANTARCTICA

Transantarctic Mts

AMUNDSEN SEA

Beardmore Glacier

Ross Ice
Shelf

Shackleton Coast

Antarctic Circle

WILKES LAND

Mt Erebus
12 447 ft △

*ROSS
SEA*

PACIFIC

OCEAN

SOUTHERN OCEAN

| 0 | 200 | 400 | 600 | 800 | 1000 miles |

| 0 | 400 | 800 | 1200 | 1600 km |

South Georgia

The lonely rugged islands that surround Antarctica are the breeding grounds for many of the sea birds attracted down to the southern oceans by the summer abundance of krill and fish.

Below *A gray-headed albatross regurgitates food to its chick. The parent catches krill, fish and squid out at sea to bring back to the nest. Albatrosses feed by settling on the water, and, in order to take off again, they spread their wings and run across the water surface into the wind.*

Right *South Georgia's climate is so severe that most of the landscape is barren rock and soil. Only in sheltered valleys is there any hint of vegetation.*

Below right *In the waters around the islands sea anemones spread their tentacles to trap the tiny organisms in the water.*

Right *Sheathbills are a perpetual nuisance for penguins on their breeding colonies. Expert thieves, sheathbills harass penguin parents as they return to feed their young and force them to regurgitate the food prematurely, which is then quickly stolen.*

Far right *Wandering albatrosses have a wingspan of 12 ft (3.5 m), the largest wingspan of any living bird. Their long narrow wings enable them to glide effortlessly for huge distances over the sea. Preferring to circle the southern oceans, they rarely approach land except to breed on the isolated islands along the Antarctic circle.*

Right inset *The sooty albatross is one of the two small species that have dark plumage. It is a skillful flier and ranges widely round the southern seas as far north as Australia and South America.*

Below *The shag is a member of the cormorant family that fishes out at sea and seldom goes near estuaries or coastal mudflats. This blue-eyed shag pair have built their nest on Signy Island in the South Orkney group just north of the long Antarctic peninsula.*

Above *Algae growing in the summer become entrapped in the ice of the glaciers, staining it with distinctive layers of color.*

Right *Only the hardiest plants can survive on the windswept islands that lie above the Antarctic Circle. This species of crowberry with its thick leaves and red fruits is found on the Falkland Islands.*

Far right *Freed of the winter covering of snow, hardy yellow lichens encrust the exposed rocks. Yet even at the height of the Antarctic summer, icicles still festoon the rock face.*

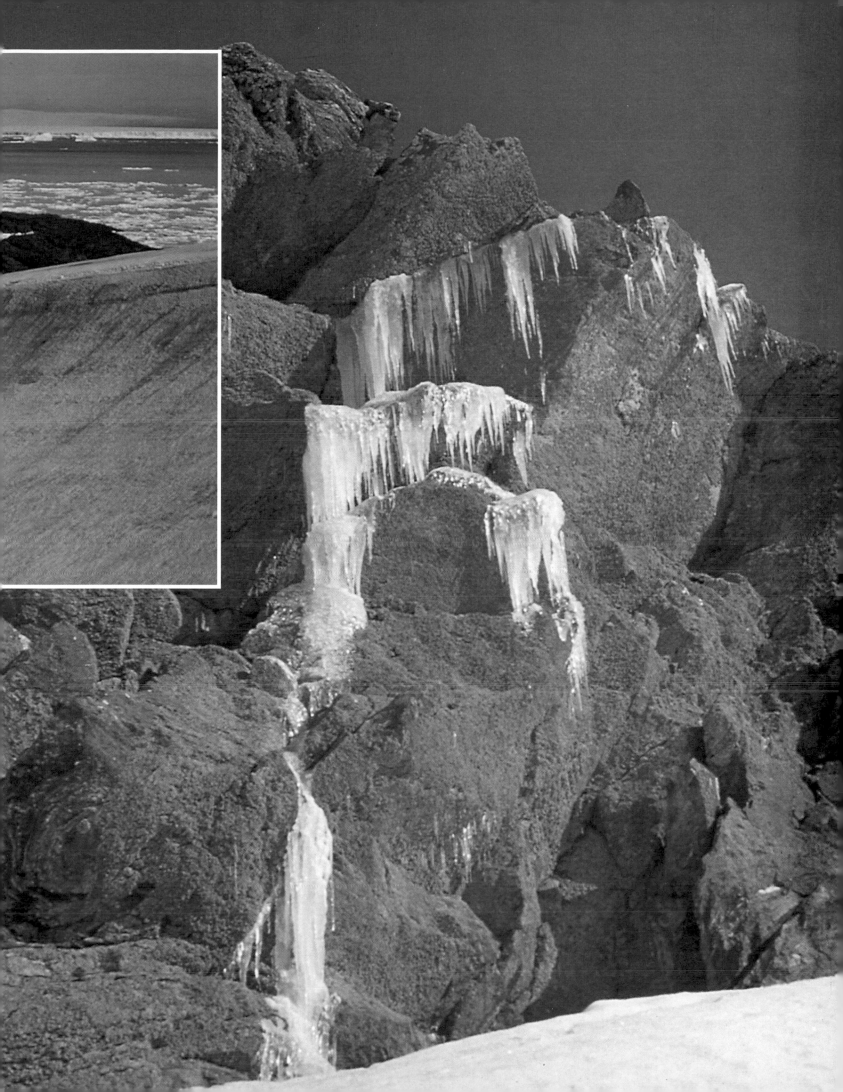

ANTARCTIC FOOD CHAIN

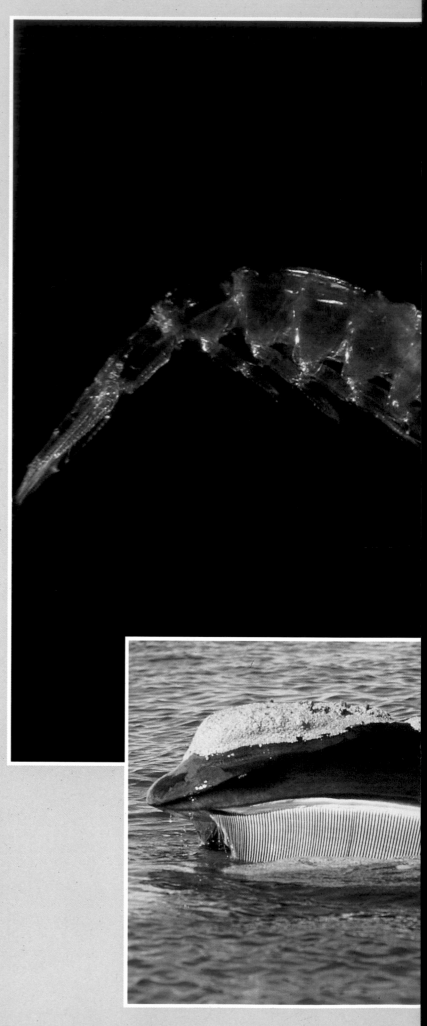

Life in the Antarctic centers round the krill. These remarkable little shrimp-like creatures feed on the abundant plankton floating in the rich Antarctic waters, and can grow from about 2 in (5 cm) to 6½ in (16 cm) in length within the short Antarctic summer. They become so numerous that huge swarms more than a mile long form near the surface, each containing several million tons of krill. It has been estimated that at the height of the summer there may be as much as 650 million tons of krill in the Antarctic.

Krill provide food for all the large Antarctic animals, either directly or indirectly. They are the staple diet of the baleen or whalebone whales (which include the fin, sei, blue, humpback and minke species). The whales graze their way steadily through the swarms of krill exposed by the melting sea ice. Baleen whales do almost all their feeding during the four months they spend in the Antarctic each year. During this period they develop sufficient quantities of fatty blubber to see them through the rest of the year when they migrate north into tropical waters where there are not such large concentrations of food.

Krill also form the staple diet of the penguins, fish and squid. These in their turn are fed on by the toothed whales (mainly sperm and killer whales as well as several species of dolphin) and by the sea birds (including albatrosses, petrels and terns). Fish, squid, penguins and krill are all part of the diet of the six species of seals that live in the Antarctic.

Between them, the sea birds and the penguins consume about 130 million tons of krill each year, while the seals account for a further 140 million tons. The whales used to take about 190 million tons, but the intensity of whaling during this century has so reduced their numbers that the figure has fallen to about 50 million tons. One indication of the decline in the numbers of whales is given by the figures for whale catches. In 1971, the fin whale catch weighed in at 500 000 tons; by 1978, it was no more than 16 000 tons.

The ecological relationships in this complex network are finely balanced. One consequence of the great reduction in the whale population has been that a great deal more krill has been available for the other species. As a result of this, the numbers of penguins and seals in particular have increased dramatically in recent years.

As the whale population declined, the krill itself began to be of interest as a potentially rich source of protein for human consumption. After some exploratory fishing in the early 1960s, the krill catch has increased steadily: by the 1980 season, it totalled 400 000 tons. The seemingly limitless processing capacity of today's giant factory ships has raised fears that the krill themselves might be over-fished. If this did happen, the entire Antarctic eco-system would collapse, for a whole variety of creatures ultimately depend on this one shrimp species. Now that the ban on whaling has succeeded in saving some of the most endangered whales from extinction, it would be ironic if we were to fail to preserve their food supply.

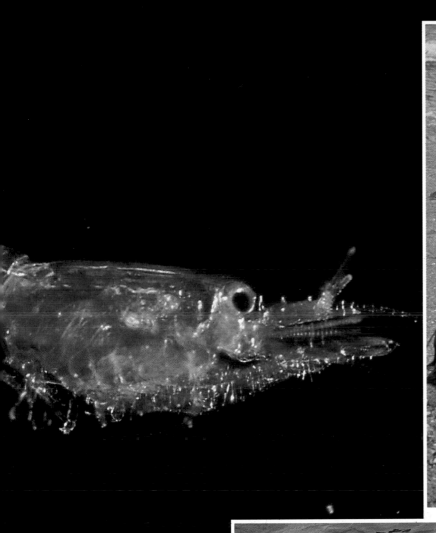

Above *The chinstrap penguin's most feared enemy, the leopard seal, is too slow on land to be a real threat.*

Above left *Krill, a deep water shrimp, is the basis of the Antarctic food chain.*

Far left *The southern right whale uses its plates of baleen to filter plankton from the sea.*

Left *Giant petrels feed on the fish that live on krill.*

Antarctic Wastes

Left *As the ice melts in the Antarctic summer the wind carves intricate sculptures that change day by day.*

Below *The haunting blue world of an ice tunnel, formed by the sealing over of a cravasse during blizzards. Ice tunnels are sometimes formed when melt water running off a glacier bores down into the ice mass.*

Below left *The southern elephant seal is the largest member of the seal family. Males (on the left) can grow to 21 ft (6.4 m) in length; females (on the right) are very much smaller. The species' name derives from the trunk-like extension of the male's nose.*
Elephant seals breed mainly on the sub-Antarctic islands as far north as the Falklands. The males engage in bloody slogging matches for the privilege of defending sectors of the beaches to which the females come to give birth. Once the pups have been weaned, the females mate before heading back out to sea until the next breeding season a year later.

Right *Icebergs are produced as the great sheets of ice break up under the action of waves during the summer months. The process is known as "calving". Because the ice sheets are flat, the icebergs often have a characteristic "table top" appearance. These slowly melt as they float northwards into warmer waters. Beautiful and exotic shapes are created by the wind, rain and waves.*

Far right *Whales can produce very deep bass notes because they are so large. Using these very low frequency sounds, they can communicate with each other over many hundreds of miles of ocean. Channels deep in the water carry these sounds in much the same way that telephone wires carry human voices. Before the oceans became polluted with the throb of ships' engines, an individual whale's deep note calls could probably be identified up to 1500 miles (2414 km) away.*

Previous page *As the summer approaches, the sea ice that has built up on the ocean surface is broken up by the action of the wind and waves. It drifts at the mercy of the currents northwards into the southern oceans as jostling pack ice. On the left of this picture can be seen the sheer face of one of the great ice barriers that fill the inner parts of the larger bays.*

Main picture *A crabeater seal (left) and a leopard seal (right) use a drifting ice floe as a raft on which to sunbathe in the unaccustomed warmth of the Antarctic summer. Leopard seals often prey on crabeaters, but out of the water the leopard seal moves too slowly to pose a serious threat.*

Inset *A crabeater seal cruises effortlessly below the ice-covered sea in search of prey. It feeds mainly on fish, squid and krill, but never on crabs, despite its name. Crabeaters are probably the most abundant species of large animal in the world: it is estimated that there are some 30 million of them in and around the Antarctic.*

Left *Paradise Bay on the Antarctic Peninsula is permanently covered by a thick ice sheet fed by a glacier from the interior. The outer seaward end of the ice sheet is broken up by the action of the waves during the Antarctic summer. The blocks of ice, some up to 30 miles (50 km) in length, drift away northwards on the currents to melt slowly as they enter the warmer waters near the tropics.*

Below left *A killer whale with its calf swims close in by the shore. Sealions look on in alarm, nervous of the most formidable killer in the southern oceans.*

Below *Weddell seals can swim under the pack ice on the frozen sea only providing they can keep breathing holes open in the ice. This one returns to its 3 week old pup left behind on the ice while it was away feeding at sea.*

PENGUINS

Penguins are restricted to the polar regions of the southern hemisphere where they live on fish and squid caught at sea. Penguins are flightless birds, their wings having adapted into stiff paddles used for diving and swimming. Although they are ungainly on land, they are extremely fast swimmers, their feathers having been modified into little furlike scales designed to enhance water-tightness and insulation.

Many penguins breed on the Antarctic coast during the brief southern summer. Some, like the royal penguin, breed in huge rookeries on the edges of the ice fields or on the rocky sub-Antarctic islands. The Adelie penguin, on the other hand, often breeds inland several miles from the sea, the birds undertaking the long journey to the sea on foot each time they want to feed.

Because the sexes look identical, elaborate courtship rituals have evolved among the penguins. Males often pick up pebbles and bring them to prospective mates to lay them at their feet. The bird's response instantly identifies its sex.

While most penguins follow the retreating food species northwards during the long Antarctic winter, a few like the emperor and king penguins remain behind to brave it out on the ice-bound continent.

The young of the king penguin are not ready to survive on their own by the time the southern winter sets in, so they are left in great huddles while the parents go out to sea. Every two or three weeks, the parents return to feed them throughout the continuous darkness of the long winter. Astonishingly, parents can recognize their own offspring among the thousands in each nursery group, although the chicks will beg food from any returning adult.

Emperor penguins breed right in the middle of the southern winter so that their large young can be fully grown before the following winter sets in. The male incubates the massive 2 lb (1 kg) egg on his feet, where it is protected from the cold and the snow by a flap of skin that hangs down from his belly. The males remain in huddles throughout the worst two months of the winter while the females are out at sea feeding more than 90 miles (145 km) away across the icy wastes. The males' brooding instinct is so strong that they have been known to incubate lumps of ice. By the time the females return, the males have lost up to half their body weight.

Left inset *A chinstrap penguin displays to its mate while "changing guard" at the nest site.*

Right *Adelie penguins jostle on the edge of the pack ice to avoid being the first into the water, alarmed by the presence of leopard seals lurking below.*

Right inset *Sitting comfortably on their parents' feet, two emperor penguin chicks meet in the breeding colony.*

Index

PICTURE CREDITS

Ardea Photographics 22-23 top, 24-25, 27, 29 top, 30-31, 38 top, 44 top, 56, 57, 59, 62-63, 67, 72-73, 75, 80, 95, 98 top, 104, 105, 106, 116-117, 118 top, 119, 120, 121, 123, 125, 126, 127, 128, 129, 130-131 bottom, 137, 139, 141 bottom, 143, 145 bottom, 153, 162-163 top, 173, 178-179, 184-185, 186, 187, 188, 190 top, 190-191, 192, 193 bottom right, 195 top, 196 left, 196-197, 198 top, 201 bottom, 202, 203, 204-205, 206-207, 209, 210-211, 212 top, 221, 226-227 **Aquila Photographic** 52 bottom, 60 left inset **Bryan and Cherry Alexander** 172-173 top, 223 **British Antarctic Survey** front endpaper, 218-219 top, 221 inset, 225 top, 237 right **Camerapix Hutchison** 36-37, 40-41, 42-43, 130-131, 138-139, 140-141, 150 top, 151, 152-153, 159 top, 163, 164-165, 172-173 bottom **Bruce Coleman Limited** contents, 10-11, 11 right, 12, 13, 26 bottom, 33, 40 top, 40 bottom, 44-45, 54, 55, 58-59, 60, 64-65, 68-69, 73, 76-77, 80-81, 82, 84, 87, 91 bottom, 93 top, 94 bottom, 96, 97, 98 middle, 101, 104-105, 109, 110, 111 bottom, 112-113, 118 bottom, 122 top, 132-133, 134, 138 bottom, 145 top, 150 bottom, 156, 160 top, 160 bottom, 161, 166 top, 166-167, 174 bottom, 182, 184, 185, 188-189, 191, 198 bottom, 199, 200, 214-215, 224-225 bottom, 234-235 **Frank Lane Picture Agency** 16 top, 26 top, 50, 61 top, 86-87, 89, 91 top, 228-229, 236-237 **Heather Angel**/Biofotos 24 bottom, 28, 42 bottom, 44 bottom, 51 top, 60-61, 65, 66 bottom, 106-107, 193 bottom left, 205, 220 bottom, 222 bottom **Robert Harding** 42 top, 74 top, 195 bottom **Eric and David Hosking** 225 bottom **The Image Bank** W von Bussche 108-109, L Brown 102-103, J H Carmichael 108, L Gordon back cover, J MaCarthy 186-187, L Lee Rue 88, C Y Shirakawa 88-89 top, A Upitis 124-125 bottom, J Anderson 170-171 **Natural Science Photos** 221 bottom **Natural History Photographic Agency** title, 6-7, 14-15, 32-33, 34-35, 37 bottom, 45, 85, 93 bottom, 100-101, 111 top, 130, 135 top, 136-137, 141 top, 154, 155, 157, 158, 160 middle, 162-163 bottom, 164 top, 167, 168-169, 171, 176-177, 194-195 top, 196 right inset, 226 bottom **Ocean Images Inc** 81, 229 **Oxford Scientific Films** 17, 18, 31, 37 top, 39, 46-47, 51, 53, 68 top, 74 bottom, 75, 83, 90-91, 99, 116, 122-123, 128, 135 bottom, 138 top, 142-143, 144, 165 top, 192-193 top, 220 top, 222-223 top, 224-225 top, 235, 237 left, back endpaper **K G Preston-Mafham**/Premaphotos 29 bottom, 72 top, 107, 159 bottom **Planet Earth Pictures** Sean Avery 38-39, Nigel Downer 66 top, Anthony Joyce 189 top, Bora Merdsoy 232-233, Colin Pennycuick 218, Jorge Provenza 124-125 top, 126-127, Christian Petron 191 inset, Nicholas Penn 183, David Rootes 232 inset, Philip Sayers 218-219 bottom, Vincent Serventy 206, Keith Scholey 15, 168, Jonathan Scott 11 left, 18 bottom, 19, 20-21, 22-23 bottom, 23 Herwarth Voigtmann 194 **Tony Stone Associates** 62, 92, 94 top, 146-147, 174 top, 174-175, 208-209, 213 **Charles Swithinbank** 227, 230-231 **Zefa** ½ title, 16 bottom, 24-25, 30, 52-53, 63, 64, 69, 70, 71, 82-83, 84-85, 96, 98-99, 100, 177, 182-183, 201 top

Multimedia Publications (UK) limited have endeavored to observe the legal requirements with regard to the rights of suppliers of photographic material.